STRUGGLING WITH
SELFISHNESS

Choosing to Look Beyond Yourself to the Heart of the Master

WOODROW KROLL

BACK TO THE BIBLE
Lincoln, Nebraska

15,000 printed to date—1996
(1160-206—15M—896)
ISBN 0-8474-1470-1

Printed in the United States of America.

ACKNOWLEDGMENTS

The struggle with selfishness—that's the saga of the patriarch Jacob and a struggle we all face at times. It would be selfish of me to allow you to think that this book was the product of my energy alone. It wasn't. As with most of our Back to the Bible publications, this was a team effort. I heartily acknowledge the time, talent and energy that my colleagues unselfishly gave to produce this book.

Allen Bean assists me in writing and research, not only for publication but also in the daily preparation for the *Back to the Bible* broadcast. His dedication to each project is a significant aid to me and is greatly appreciated. In addition to her usual duties, my secretary, Cathy Strate, coordinated broadcast and writing schedules, double-checked Scripture references and made helpful suggestions to the project as a whole. Rachel Derowitsch capably edits all of Back to the Bible's publications, checking spelling, syntax, grammar, etc. But equally important are her editorial suggestions, which always result in a better publication. And Kim Johnson is our creative person who gives vision to the cover design concept and always comes up with a winner.

Special thanks to Bob Peterson, who heads our printing department, and his team of professionals for the quality work they do in printing, cutting and binding each book. Their work is a constant source of delight to me. And since the substance of this book was first the substance of a series of radio broadcasts, I want to thank

Don Hawkins, producer of the *Back to the Bible* broadcast, and his engineering team, especially Neal Thompson and Kirk Chestnut. These and many others labor unselfishly, through a variety of media, to bring the message of God's Word to hearts and lives around the world. Thanks to you for being one of those.

It is my prayer that as you read these pages you will seriously challenge your personal life. Ask God to bring to light any hidden areas of selfishness. Ask Him to use the saga of Jacob to instruct and encourage you in your own struggle with selfishness. That's one of the most unselfish things any of us can do.

CONTENTS

INTRODUCTION

I encountered an interesting list the other day. It suggests some things you can do that guarantee you will be perfectly miserable and stay that way. Since none of us desires unhappiness, I thought I'd share some of these items. In order to be miserable, all you have to do is:

1. Think about yourself.
2. Talk about yourself.
3. Use the personal pronoun I as often as possible in your conversations.
4. Listen greedily to what people say about you.
5. Demand agreement with your views on everything.
6. Sulk if people aren't grateful to you for favors shown them.
7. Expect to be appreciated.
8. Be suspicious.
9. Be jealous and envious.
10. Never forget a criticism.

If I were to sum up this list in one word, it would be *selfishness*. Some people have said that selfishness is the root cause of all the world's unhappiness. I can't disagree with that. Selfishness is inherent in everyone. Every child is born with the assumption that the world revolves around him. Nearly the first word out of his mouth is *mine*. You don't have to teach a child how to be selfish; he comes by it naturally, taking after his parents. One of the primary functions of godly parenting is to turn our self-centered tots into "other-centered" adults, and that takes a heavy dose of unselfish maturity—something not all adults possess.

Many people become adults physically but remain self-centered toddlers emotionally. Undoubtedly you have met folks like that. They are everywhere. You also can identify them in the Bible, and Jacob is a good example.

This man was one of the great patriarchs, a father of his country, a champion in Israelite history. In fact, if it were not for Jacob, there would be no Israelite history. But Jacob struggled with selfishness all his life. Even his birth had a tinge of selfishness in it. He was born only a few moments after his twin brother, Esau, yet as he came out of his mother's womb "his hand took hold of Esau's heel" (Gen. 25:26). This free birth ride was the reason he was named Jacob, which means "supplanter" or "one who takes another's place." From his birth, Jacob was selfishly attempting to displace his twin brother.

When we next meet him as a young adult, he is supplanting his brother in the privileges of the birthright (Gen. 25:29-34). Later, in Genesis 27:19-29, he takes his brother's place in receiving the family blessing. Jacob was determined to come out on top no matter what he had to do or whom he had to hurt in the process. One of the last times we meet Jacob he is sending his sons back to Egypt to get food, even though they were convinced that they would forfeit their lives in the process (Gen. 43).

Without question, some of the blame for Jacob's struggle with selfishness must be laid at the feet of his parents, Isaac and Rebekah. They made the classic

8

parenting *faux pas* of playing favorites. Isaac had a preference for Esau, the macho hunter, a man among men. But Rebekah preferred the stay-at-home Jacob, a man about the house. This turned brothers into competitors and the consequence was a no-holds-barred rivalry.

But ultimately Jacob could not blame his parents. He had to take responsibility for his own actions. Before his parents practiced any parenting, Jacob was practicing selfishness. And long after his parents were gone, he was still acting out his selfish desires. His relationships with his brother as well as with his uncle, Laban, his wives, Rachel and Leah, and his children were marred by selfishness. Jacob left a trail of broken hearts and twisted lives in his wake.

Things haven't changed much since the days of the patriarch. Today our society is experiencing an enormous surge in selfishness. Sometimes it's so subtle that we barely notice it. For example, think how magazine titles have changed over time. Years ago one of the most popular magazines was called *Life*. Then one came on the scene called *People*. This was followed by *Us*. Now we have a magazine called *Self*. Is this just a coincidence? I don't think so. It's symptomatic of encroaching selfishness.

Andrew Peyton Thomas, writing in *The Wall Street Journal*, observed, "If the source of America's social disintegration is to be pinpointed so that it might be remedied, honesty compels us not to neglect this issue [selfishness]. . . . Self-centeredness and its related vices—crime, illegitimacy, child neglect—are exploding in America because, after centuries of Western philosophy devoted to the purpose, Americans are glorifying extreme individualism beyond healthy limits, and beyond anything ever experienced by another national culture."[1]

Many parents today appear to be more concerned about their own comfort and pleasure than their children's future. The Council on Families in America claims that the children of the present parenting generation "are the first in our nation's history to be less well off—psychologically, socially, economically and morally—than their parents were at the same age. . . . Child well-being is deteriorating, as reflected in statistics on everything from poverty and substance abuse to depression, homicide and suicide."[2] Chuck Klein, executive director of Campus Crusade's Student Venture, claims, "This generation [of young people] is the most attacked and abused of the 13 generations we've had in America."[3]

The problem is selfishness. It motivates a grandmother to fatally stab her seven-year-old granddaughter because she was misbehaving.[4] It prompts a single mother to drown her two small sons because her boyfriend didn't want to be bothered with them.[5] And it results in a father strangling his three-year-old son because he wouldn't stop crying.[6]

While most of us stop far short of such horrendous crimes, we are still frequently guilty of selfishness. We insist on our rights. We have the right to read the paper for half an hour without interruption. We have the right to play a weekly round of golf, go fishing or "shop 'till we drop." And if our rights are violated, we get angry. We want no one to infringe on what is ours.

So, is it a losing battle? Are there ways to gain victory over our struggle with selfishness? Or are we just too selfish to want to defeat selfishness? Answering these questions is what this book is all about. All of us struggle with selfishness, but too often we struggle in a losing battle. Jacob was like that. Yet what we can learn from this supplanter will help us recognize our own selfishness and help us overcome it. The Bible has the answer; Jacob provides the example; you and I need to apply the insight that comes from Jacob's life and his struggle with selfishness.

1 Andrew Peyton Thomas, "Can we ever go back?" *The Wall Street Journal*, August 9, 1995.

2 William Raspberry, "The disastrous effect of divorce on kids," *Indianapolis Star*, April 4, 1995, p. A-7.

3 *National & International Report*, January 8, 1996.

4 "Grandma charged in stabbing of girl," *San Francisco Examiner*, May 9, 1995, via the Internet.

5 Barbara Ehrenreich, "Susan Smith corrupted by love?" *Time*, August 7, 1995, p. 78.

6 "Father sentenced in abuse of son," *Lincoln Star*, May 12, 1995, p. 29.

Chapter 1

CHOOSING THE MORAL WAY

———— ✑ ————

Some moral obligations are required by law. If a state patrolman stops you for going over the speed limit, he's not going to accept your argument that you have no moral obligation to go slower. In fact, he will probably write you a ticket to prove that you do.

Other moral obligations are just as real, but not so enforceable. These are not codified into a set of legal laws but exist instead in our hearts and conscience. Yet they are as important as the ones found written on paper.

The Bible says much about moral needs. Some have become a part of our legal system (thou shalt not kill, thou shalt not steal), but even more are part of our lives simply because God has told us that they are the right thing to do. Perhaps these are the ones we struggle with the most. Our natural selfishness says, "There's no law that says I have to do this," while God's Spirit says, "This is right—do it." The struggle with selfishness is always a struggle with doing what we know is right even with no benefit to us.

Jacob was faced with such a choice in Genesis 25:29-30: "Now Jacob cooked a stew; and Esau came in from the field, and he was weary. And Esau said to Jacob, 'Please feed me with that same red stew, for I am weary.' Therefore his name was called Edom."[1]

Helping people in distress is one of those moral obligations found frequently in Scripture. God says in

13

Deuteronomy 15:11, "For the poor will never cease from the land; therefore I command you, saying, 'You shall open your hand wide to your brother, to your poor and your needy, in your land.'" Leviticus 19:9-10 says, "When you reap the harvest of your land, you shall not wholly reap the corners of your field when you reap, nor shall you gather the gleanings of your harvest. . . . You shall leave them for the poor and for the stranger: I am the LORD your God.'"

Esau was in need. He had been out in the fields working hard, hunting to provide the meat that his father loved so much. He hadn't had breakfast or lunch, and he was famished. Jacob, meanwhile, had stayed at home thumbing through his cookbook and found a recipe for a delicious lentil stew, which he made.

When Esau came to him, Jacob had no legal obligation to provide for his brother. The fact that his brother was faint with hunger was not his problem. And that's where selfishness overtook him. What he did was immoral. Jacob refused to meet Esau's need unless he could receive some payment first. So he demanded Esau's birthright.

The importance of birthrights

This may make little impression on you because birthrights don't exist in our culture. But to Esau and Jacob it was extremely important. The birthright (*bekowrah* in Hebrew) was a privilege extended normally to the firstborn of the family. Deuteronomy 21:17 says that the father shall give his firstborn "a double portion of all that he has, for he is the beginning of his strength; the right of the firstborn [*bekowrah*] is his." Not only did the birthright bestow a double portion of material possessions upon the owner, it also gave him the right to represent the family in all the legal, social and religious affairs of society. Thus, there was a prestigious as well as financial advantage to being the possessor of the birthright. But for the descendants of Abraham there was something even more important connected to the birthright—the covenant promise.

In Genesis 15 God made a promise to Abraham: "Then He brought him outside and said, 'Look now toward heaven, and count the stars if you are able to number them.' And He said to him, 'So shall your descendants be.' And he believed in the LORD, and He accounted it to him for righteousness. Then He said to him, 'I am the LORD, who brought you out of Ur of the Chaldeans, to give you this land to inherit it'" (vv. 5-7). This covenant promise is repeated in Genesis 22:15-18: "Then the Angel of the LORD called to Abraham a second time out of heaven, and said: 'By Myself I have sworn, says the LORD, because you have done this thing, and have not withheld your son, your only son; in blessing I will bless you, and in multiplying I will multiply your descendants as the stars of the heaven and as the sand which is on the seashore; and your descendants shall possess the gate of their enemies. In your seed all the nations of the earth shall be blessed, because you have obeyed My voice.'"

God promised to make a nation out of Abraham and his descendants, give them a land and through them bring forth a descendant who would bless all the nations (which was fulfilled through the Messiah). But since this would take centuries to fulfill, the promise had to be taken by faith. This promise was an important part of the birthright. It had passed from Abraham to Isaac and would have passed from Isaac to Esau—but for the selfishness of Jacob.

That bowl of lentil soup had a high price tag—but Esau paid it. He thought more of his momentary satisfaction than he did of all that would be his in the future. He preferred the here and now to the somewhat vague and uncertain future. He chose that which could be seen and felt over that which had to be taken by faith.

Esau failed to respect the value of his birthright, but Jacob also failed by selfishly refusing to meet a moral need without requiring anything in return. Jacob knew that he was asking an exorbitant price for a bowl of soup, yet his selfish heart said, "I can't just give it to him; I've got to get something out of this"; and he greedily went after the greatest thing his brother would ever have—his birthright.

And the beat goes on

Are things much different in the business world today? With today's pressure on bottom-line profits and pleasing stockholders, there's little motivation for companies to meet the moral needs of their employees. The necessity to downsize and cut costs has created a moral dilemma, especially for Christian-owned companies. There is no legal law that says a corporation has to make special efforts to help those caught in these circumstances, but don't we have a moral obligation to do what is right? Even in downsizing, we must treat our employees ethically. Downsizing may be a fact of life today, but people who lose their jobs need to be viewed as friends and colleagues, not as "excess baggage" to whom we have no moral obligation. How you provide for those who are severed from your payroll tells a lot about your organization, and about you.

Even the church can be guilty of this immoral behavior. In his book *Burden of a Secret*, Dr. Jimmy Allen relates his personal story of truth and mercy in the face of AIDS. Dr. Allen was well known in the Southern Baptist denomination and served several times as president of the Southern Baptist Convention in the United States. His 13-year-old grandson, Matthew, contracted HIV and consequently AIDS through a blood transfusion that was given to Matthew's mother before he was born. Matthew's brother, Brian, also contracted AIDS and died in 1986. His mother, Lydia, died of AIDS in 1992. Yet when the family turned to the church for help, they were rejected. Dr. Allen relates in his book the sad truth that church after church refused to let Matthew into Sunday school; Christian school after Christian school refused to enroll him. As in the case of Jacob, here was potential for significant mercy, but instead the response was sinful selfishness.

It's true that we don't understand all that we would like to about AIDS, and we tend to fear that which we don't understand. But fear is often nothing more than selfishness in disguise. We should understand enough about our moral obligation to lend assistance whatever the cost. God's Word says, "Therefore, as we have opportunity, let us do good to all, especially to those who are of the household of faith" (Gal. 6:10). Selfishness shouldn't be allowed to keep us from meeting a moral need.

Sometimes when the church or other Christian organization does help, it attaches strings to its aid. Before Jacob could respond to Esau's need, he wanted to make sure that he was going to get something out of it. Before we respond to someone's need in our community, are we tempted to see what's in it for us? Do we make sure all the cameras are there so we can get some good publicity out of our aid? Or do we expect the person we helped to attend our church now? If this is true, does this make us any different from the hypocrites whom Jesus condemned because they selfishly made a great show out of their piousness (Matt. 6:1-6)?

The moral responsibility to help those in need not only belongs to Christian organizations but filters down to the individual as well. Where there is a need, it is the responsibility of every moral person not only to be aware of that need but in some way to respond to it. Job was criticized by his friends who claimed he had done nothing that would demonstrate his claim that he was righteous (Job 29). How did Job defend himself against these charges? Not with philosophical or spiritual arguments, but with examples of his social actions. He said, "Have I not wept for him who was in trouble? Has not my soul grieved for the poor?" (Job 30:25). You might say, "Well, grief is one thing, but did Job ever help the poor? Who would not claim to be grieved over the poor?"

But Job's inward grief was translated into outward actions. In chapter 31 he said, "If I have kept the poor from their desire, or caused the eyes of the widow to fail, or eaten my morsel by myself, so that the fatherless could not eat of it . . . ; if I have seen anyone perish for lack of clothing, or any poor man without covering; . . . then let my arm fall from my shoulder, let my arm be torn from the socket" (vv. 16-17, 19, 22). In essence Job said: "Look, I don't have a thing to worry about when I stand before my Father because I have responded with sensitivity to the moral needs around me and asked nothing in return." Those are pretty tough words if you have lived in a struggle with selfishness. Obviously, Job understood the morality of helping those who are in need. He saw a moral need and made it his moral duty.

How well do you respond to the physical need of those you encounter? If you see someone who is hungry, do you give him food? Do you expect something in return? If you have a family in your church who needs a place to stay for awhile, do you offer your spare room? Do you make them promise to pay rent after they get back on their feet? Is your moral compass set at true north, or are you working an angle with your helpfulness?

Selfishness in the family

What makes Jacob's selfishness even more repugnant is that he refused to meet the need of his own brother. Sometimes we respond to the needs of others more readily than we respond to the needs of our family. An overworked minister habitually told his congregation that if they needed a pastoral visit to drop a note in the offering plate. One evening after the service he discovered a note that said, "I am one of your loneliest members and heaviest contributors. May I have a visit tomorrow evening?" It was signed by his wife.

Do you have family members who need you? Maybe they need you spiritually, emotionally or even financially. Will they fare any better than Esau did in his need? Jacob refused to meet his moral responsibility to help his brother. Is that failure happening all over again in your experience? Jacob turned his back on Esau until he got something out of him. What drove him to such callousness? Pure selfishness. What keeps you from helping your family?

Morality is not always legislated—sometimes it is

simply the product of the Holy Spirit at work in our lives. We can choose to do just what we have to. That keeps us legal but it also makes us selfish. God says we need to go beyond the law and choose to live morally in our relationships with others. Our struggle with selfishness often forces us to choose between others' needs and our welfare. When it does, do we choose a birthright or our brother?

---

1 The stew ("pottage" in the King James Version) was probably made of red lentils. The Hebrew word for *red* is *'adom*, which is why Esau was given the nickname Edom. Later his descendants founded a nation, which also was called Edom.

Chapter 2

Choosing the Honest Way

——— ✎ ———

As a buyer for J.C. Penny Co., Jimmy Locklear controlled the spending of millions of dollars a year. Since his salary was $56,000, in 1988 Locklear decided to pad his income by peddling his influence. He sold crucial information to some suppliers and manufacturers' representatives, such as the amount of their competitor's bids. To others, he blatantly sold the promise of large orders. In exchange, some vendors handed him cash; others wrote checks to front companies he set up. Over four years, Jimmy Locklear supplemented his salary with as much as $1.5 million in bribes and kickbacks.[1] I wish I could say that this is an exception, but that's not the case. According to *Bottom Line/Business*, fraudulent business practices cost companies in the United States about $400 billion in 1995.[2]

But dishonesty doesn't stop with the corporate world. It permeates every part of our society, including the health and welfare institutions of our government. A secret witness told a panel of United States Senators that "some hospitals illegally, and with little fear of getting caught, bill Medicare for experiments with new medical devices." In fact, he said, "Physicians go so far as to joke of the government's ineptness to investigate and prosecute the fraud." The General Accounting Office, which acts as a watchdog for this sort of thing, says that Medicare losses caused by fraud may total as much as $17 billion.[3] *The Wall Street Journal* reported that food

21

stamp fraud now costs the government as much as $1 billion each year.[4] So who pays for this? You do. American taxpayers lose billions of dollars a year to selfish, dishonest swindlers. The same is true in every country in the world.

A well-known German TV producer, Michael Born, was accused of "faking" TV documentaries by hiring actors and using friends to create stories that he thought would sell. In one instance he hired Albanians to pose as Kurdish fighters. On another occasion he interviewed friends and said they were Austrian terrorists. What may be most disturbing is that Born claims, "I am only a small cog in the machine . . . many others are selling doctored news as well."[5]

Deception even stains the reputation of the educational community. Columnist Cal Thomas quoted the *Boston Globe*, which claimed that 50 percent of college students cheat; for high school students it's 75 percent.[6] A survey conducted by *Reader's Digest* reported that 76 percent of college students surveyed admitted they had cheated on tests while in high school and few, if any, expressed any remorse at their behavior. What may be more shocking is that the teachers and administrators in America's public school system also regularly cheated. Since they are evaluated by the achievements of their students, it's to the administration's advantage to make it appear that their pupils are performing well. In one California high school a 1994 audit uncovered more than 600 changed grades and other discrepancies in student transcripts.[7]

What does all this mean? We live in a society of cheaters, a society of people who routinely deceive others because they are selfish and want what's best for them. If it means lying to the government, stealing from their company or cheating on exams, so be it. The important element is taking care of one's self. Cheaters all over the world are struggling with selfishness.

But deception is not a 20th century phenomenon. It may be getting more common these days, but turn back to the Bible and you'll find there were some pretty good deceivers in biblical times as well. Perhaps the most prominent deceiver recorded in the Bible is Jacob.

Jacob struggled with selfishness all his life, and the further we progress in his story, the more opportunities he had to demonstrate his selfishness. Invariably, selfishness gives rise to deceit. Jacob's selfishness even drove him to deceive his own family. In Genesis 27:1-4 we read:

> Now it came to pass, when Isaac was old and his eyes were so dim that he could not see, that he called Esau his older son and said to him, "My son." And he answered him, "Here I am." Then he said, "Behold now, I am old. I do not know the day of my death. Now therefore, please take your weapons, your quiver and your bow, and go out to the field and hunt game for me. And make me savory food, such as I love, and bring it to me that I may eat, that my soul may bless you before I die.

Although Isaac was speaking to his favored son, Esau, in these verses, this conversation set the stage for the deception by Jacob, Rebekah's favored son. Unbeknown to Isaac or Esau, Rebekah overheard his instructions.

Immediately she relayed this information to her beloved son, and together they began to plot how they might outwit the elderly man.

God had told Rebekah before Jacob and Esau were born, "Two nations are in your womb, two peoples shall be separated from your body; one people shall be stronger than the other, and the older shall serve the younger" (Gen. 25:23). But this promise was not sufficient for her or her son. Instead of trusting God to work out the details, Rebekah and Jacob decided to take matters into their own hands. Apparently, selfishness ran in their family. By hook or by crook, they were going to make sure Jacob was the preeminent son. Their selfishness drove them to stoop to dishonesty. They were no better than Jimmy Locklear.

Deceiving the elderly

The deception of older people is becoming an increasing burden on my heart. It's not new, of course—we see it happening in the story of Jacob—but it is on the rise today. The first four verses of Genesis 27 depict Jacob as so selfish he is willing to take advantage of his elderly father to get what he wants. Twice in these verses we are told that Jacob's father was old. In that patriarchal society, age usually fostered respect. But selfishness skews society, and respect gave way to deception.

Today people are living longer, and that means more and more individuals fall into the category of the elderly. By 2025 at the latest, 20 percent of Americans will be 65 or older; by 2040, that number will increase to 25 percent.[8] The older we grow, the greater the opportunities for others to take advantage of us. For example, 72-year-old Edward Tafoya from Bellflower, California, and his wife, Julia, were approached at a shopping center by a Spanish-speaking woman. The woman claimed she had a winning California Lotto ticket but couldn't cash it because she was an illegal alien. She convinced the couple to "buy" the ticket for $11,000. Once she had the money she left the pair holding a sealed envelope. What was inside the envelope? Not Lotto tickets but Lotto receipts marked "Not for Sale."[9] Scam artists are more than willing to deceive the elderly to satisfy their selfishness.

But surely you wouldn't guess such deception could ever happen in the Christian community. Guess again. From 1989 to May 1995, John G. Bennet Jr., a professing Christian, bilked not only hundreds of Christians organizations but a number of elderly philanthropists out of millions of dollars through his Foundation for New Era Philanthropy. Jim Reapsome, missionary strategist and editor of a newsletter called *World Pulse*, claims that a major reason many fell victim to the fraudulent foundation was "because the man who ran it came with impeccable Christian credentials."[10] When Jesus said the Pharisees had made God's house "a den of thieves" (Matt. 21:13), he could have been speaking of the 20th century as well.

Most people who are elderly or have aging parents are keenly aware of the dangers of being cheated out of a life's savings by the selfishness of deceivers. We read about it in the newspaper every day. We even read about it in the Bible. Jacob was not the first person to deceive the elderly, nor the last. But surely the selfishness that drives a person to deceive his elderly father is the worst selfishness of all.

Deceiving the physically infirmed

Not only did Jacob take advantage of his father's age, he also took advantage of his father's physical condition. It was like adding injury to insult. Genesis 27:1 reveals that Isaac's eyes were "dim." In order to deceive his father into thinking he was Esau, who was a hairy man, Jacob, under the advise of his mother, covered his hands and arms with goat skins. Knowing his father was dependent on feel, he rightfully concluded Isaac wouldn't be able to tell him apart from hairy Esau. Jacob's selfishness had so hardened his heart that he was willing to use his father's physical infirmities as a means to deceive him.

Age frequently brings weakness and physical ailments. Virginia Alvin and Glenn Silverstein make these observations about aging: "The heart muscle is not as efficient at 80. The heart pumps about 30 percent less blood than it did at 30. Typically a person loses a quarter to half an inch of height with each ten years after the age of 30. In the years between ages 30 and 75, the body may lose 20 to 30 percent of its cells. These tiny, microscopic losses and errors add up to produce changes in the body's tissues and organs."[11] These changes manifest themselves in the loss of hearing, eyesight and even taste. Many of us have already experienced these changes. Such ailments put us at risk for being deceived.

Cancer, multiple sclerosis, accidents and numerous other debilitating problems also can cause a person to be vulnerable to the deception of selfish people. The owner of a cancer clinic in Brownsville, Texas, drew patients from all over the country with his Digitron D Spectometer device and Larginine serum that supposedly cured cancer. Patients paid up to $3,000 each for the purported cures.[12] Another "miracle cure" that is spreading through the country is the Kombucha "Tea" craze. It is claimed that four ounces of this elixir, three times a day before meals, will cure everything from wrinkles to AIDS.

It's sad when age and illness become vehicles of deception. Yet selfish hearts know neither pity nor honor. Like Jacob, selfish individuals will stop at nothing to get their way even if it means taking advantage of a person's disabilities. Taking advantage of the elderly and the infirm is part of the deceitful culture of our day—and only seems to be getting worse.

Deceiving the vulnerable

Isaac had a personal vulnerability. The chink in his armor was his taste for food—but not just any food. Isaac had a personal weakness for the savory taste of venison. Jacob recognized he could take his father's vulnerability and turn it to his advantage. Rebekah had Jacob take a lamb from his flocks, which she prepared for Isaac in a special way so that he thought he was eating venison. Then Jacob brought the food to Isaac. His father said, "'Bring it near to me, and I will eat of my son's game, so that my soul may bless you.' So he brought it near to him, and he ate; and he brought him wine, and he drank" (Gen. 27:25). Jacob cared nothing about pleasing his father; he cared everything about using his father's vulnerability to feed his selfish desires.

Many of us have food weaknesses. For me it's chocolate—good, wholesome, "calorie-free" chocolate. I never met a piece of chocolate I didn't like. My motto is "Chocolate: it's not just for breakfast anymore." Of course, in and of itself, a weakness is not a sin. There was nothing wrong with Isaac enjoying a tasty piece of meat or me a piece of dark, rich chocolate. But these weaknesses can provide an inroad for personal sin or for selfish people to take advantage of us.

Other people are vulnerable in their emotions. Perhaps they are easily moved to sorrow or pity. Con artists quickly identify these weaknesses and use them to get what they want. One con man made himself up as a pregnant woman and approached an elderly man with a tearful story of how "she" needed an abortion. The elderly man was persuaded to give $200 toward the procedure. Two days later the con artist returned to the victim and requested an additional $500 because the "pregnancy" involved triplets. Finding the elderly person easy prey, the "woman" returned a few days later claiming the check had been lost and received yet another check for $500. The deceiver returned a third time asking for a check for $800 to hold a used car with the promise that the check would not actually be cashed. It was cashed the same day. The elderly man was then persuaded to deliver $1,500 for bond money to have "her" released from jail. This incredible scam would have continued had not bank officials become suspicious and notified the police. Officers arrested the con man but the money was long gone.

God instructs us to be compassionate and generous. James, the brother of Jesus, said, "If a brother or sister is naked and destitute of daily food, and one of you says to them, 'Depart in peace, be warmed and filled,' but you do not give them the things which are needed for the body, what does it profit?" (James 2:15-16). The apostle Paul declared, "But this I say: He who sows sparingly will also reap sparingly, and he who sows bountifully will also reap bountifully" (2 Cor. 9:6). But along with these instructions Jesus commanded, "Behold, I send you out as sheep in the midst of wolves. Therefore be wise as serpents and harmless as doves" (Matt. 10:16).

Be on your guard, especially in those areas where you know you're vulnerable. Set guidelines and rules for yourself that you refuse to violate. For example, if you have low sales resistance, determine that you will not buy from a phone solicitor or door-to-door salesperson without checking first with someone you trust and then only after a 24-hour "cooling off" period to make sure your purchase is a wise one. If it has to be purchased "right now" in order to get the "good deal," then tell them you'll have to pass. You won't be sorry. If the opportunity is legitimate, it will be there tomorrow as surely as it is today.

The saga of Jacob's selfishness always traveled the low road, but it was never lower than when he took advantage of the age, infirmity and vulnerability of his father. Selfishness is a terrible thing. It makes people do dreadful things, even people who are related to us. If you think you may be vulnerable to the selfishness of others, especially if those others are people you know well and trust explicitly, what should you do?

Get educated or get taken

In an editorial entitled "Get educated or get taken," Jim Reapsome wrote, "Religious con artists know that Christians are more inclined than others to be charitable. They know certain stories will pull on the heartstrings and checkbooks of Christians. Stories of starving people and abandoned babies rack up huge piles of loot. When the stories come from the lips of 'natives' themselves, they are even more likely to draw a response. Stories about fast-closing 'open doors,' thousands of converts, and new churches will induce generous offerings. Religious cheaters create apocalyptic crises faster than bad breath ruins romances on TV commercials."[13] Mr. Reapsome appeals in the name of good stewardship for Christians to lose some of their naivete.

Unfortunately, not too many of us—whether churches or individuals—want to make the effort to get educated. Some people find it easier and perhaps "more spiritual" simply to take the word of those who say they represent the needy. Furthermore, they find it difficult to believe that someone who claims to be a Christian could be so calloused or so crooked as to take advantage of their brothers and sisters in Christ. The unwillingness to take the time and effort to do even minor investigative work has resulted in Christians paying a high price for their laziness. Money that could have been used to support a legitimate missions project or help those truly in need has gone instead to line the pockets of selfish deceivers.

Getting educated doesn't mean you have to earn a degree in sleuthing. You don't even have to have the wit and wisdom of Sherlock Holmes. It simply means asking some hard questions and demanding some straight answers in return. Remember, unless you're there when the photos were taken, you can't trust pictures and testimonies—lots of new converts standing in front of new churches could really be old Christians standing in front of old churches. It's hard to tell the difference if you're thousands of miles away. As for "critical" crises, who says so? Maybe just the promoter.

Ask for some type of verification of deeds done. This

should be conducted by an outside, independent source. When you get appeals for ministry in far-off places, Jim Reapsome suggests that you fax or E-mail someone you know on the scene. Check it out before you give. Beware of people who claim to be the "only group" doing this or that. Such holy skepticism is simply being as wise as a serpent, while remaining as harmless as a dove.

It's a shame that we have to be so cautious in the area of giving, but deception is always close at hand. Make sure you are dealing with people of integrity, not people like the selfish Jacob. I've often said that at Back to the Bible we cherish integrity more than anything else. It can take more than 50 years to build integrity but only a few minutes to lose it.

Selfishness is everywhere in our world today. Jesus said of the latter days, "And because lawlessness will abound, the love of many will grow cold" (Matt. 24:12). Those words certainly describe our day and age. Selfishness can even creep into the lives of God's people. Jacob was one of the Patriarchs (along with Abraham and Isaac), and yet he was an incredibly selfish man. He took advantage of his father because he didn't trust God to give him what He promised. You and I need to be kind and generous but also exceedingly wise, because it's possible for us to be deceived from inside the Christian community itself or, worse, from within our own family. Whenever selfishness raises its ugly head, deception is not far behind.

1 *The Wall Street Journal,* February 7, 1995, p. 1.

2 Daniel Karson, "Fraud prevention," *Bottom Line/Business,* March 1, 1996, p. 3.

3 Diane Duston, "Secret witness tells of Medicare fraud," *Lincoln Journal Star,* February 15, 1996, p. A-5.

4 John R. Emshwiller, "Hot special at small stores: food-stamp fraud," *The Wall Street Journal,* June 1, 1995, p. B-1.

5 Terrence Petty, "German TV producer caught in 'news' hoax," *Lincoln Journal Star,* February 15, 1996.

6 Cal Thomas, Friendship Banquet, Lincoln Christian Foundation, Lincoln, Nebraska, February 27, 1996.

7 "Cheating in school," *Indianapolis Star,* February 23, 1996, p. A-8.

8 Peter G. Peterson, "Will America grow up before it grows old?" *The Atlantic Monthly,* April 30, 1996, p. 1, via the Internet.

9 Tina Griego, "Elderly couple fleeced of $11,000 for fake Lotto ticket," *Los Angeles Times,* August 3, 1990, p. B-4.

10 Jim Reapsome, "Now that we've lost millions . . ." *World Pulse,* June 25, 1995, p. 8.

11 Virginia Alvin and Glenn Silverstein, *Venture,* January/February 1983, pp. 11-13.

12 Paul Ciotti, "Cancer clinic scam brings 2-year term," *Los Angeles Times,* December 17, 1991, p. A-3.

13 Jim Reapsome, "Get educated or get taken," *World Pulse,* December 1, 1995, p. 8.

Chapter 3

Choosing the Righteous Way

In his book *Healing for Damaged Emotions*, David Seamands tells of the trauma of his open heart surgery. Before the operation a nurse came into the room to visit and told him to take her hand and hold it. "Now," she said, "during surgery tomorrow you will be disconnected from your heart and you will be kept alive only by certain machines. When the operation is over you will be reconnected and you will eventually awaken in a special recovery room. But you will be immobile for as long as six hours. You may be unable to move, or speak, or to even open your eyes, but you will be perfectly conscious and you will hear and know everything that is going on around you. During those six hours I will be at your side and I will hold your hand exactly as I am doing now. I will stay with you until you are fully recovered. Although you may feel absolutely helpless, when you feel my hand, you will know that I am with you and I will not leave."[1]

Seamands says that it happened exactly as the nurse told him. He could do nothing. "But," he said, "I could feel the nurse's hand in my hand for hours. And that made all the difference."

Righteousness is that condition in which we once again are restored to the presence of God. His hand firmly grasps our own, and that connectedness for which we were created is restored. Mankind was not made to be estranged from God but to have fellowship with Him. Genesis 3:8 records, "And they heard the sound of the LORD God walking in the garden

33

in the cool of the day, and Adam and his wife hid themselves from the presence of the LORD God among the trees of the garden." This verse reveals two facts. First, God was accustomed to fellowshipping with His creation. They were connected. Man was created to enjoy the glory of God's presence. Second, sin broke that fellowship. Immediately after their sin, Adam and Eve sensed there was something wrong; something had been lost. Their connection with God had been "unplugged." Instead of enjoying His company, they "hid themselves from the presence of the LORD."

Is there any way we can get plugged back into fellowship with God? Not on our own, but God has made a way. When we receive Christ as our Savior we are declared by God and treated by Him as if we are righteous. We enjoy the righteousness of Christ spread over us like a cloak. We have a "right relationship" renewed with God. We are reconnected to our Creator. Once again we can experience God's presence in our lives, and that makes all the difference.

The blessing of His presence

In one sense it is impossible to escape the presence of God. The psalmist knew this. He asked, "Where can I go from Your Spirit? Or where can I flee from Your presence? If I ascend into heaven, You are there; if I make my bed in hell, behold, You are there. If I take the wings of the morning, and dwell in the uttermost parts of the sea, even there Your hand shall lead me, and Your right hand shall hold me" (Ps. 139:7-10).

God is present everywhere. One of the great truths about God is that He is omnipresent, everywhere equally present at the same time. You can't avoid God's presence, but sometimes our relationship with Him makes us wish we could. Those who live wicked lives do not relish the thought that God is present everywhere as they engage in their wickedness. God's omnipresence brings fear and trepidation to many. In the end days, we are told,

> The kings of the earth, the great men, the rich men, the commanders, the mighty men, every slave and every free man, hid themselves in the caves and in the rocks of the mountains, and said to the mountains and rocks, "Fall on us and hide us from the face of Him who sits on the throne and from the wrath of the Lamb! For the great day of His wrath has come, and who is able to stand?" (Rev. 6:15-17).

In the day of judgment, those who brag of their independence from God today will fall in fear before the knowledge that He has observed every wicked thing they have done.

For those who are restored to righteousness, however, their reaction is quite different. The psalmist said, "In Your presence is fullness of joy; at Your right hand are pleasures forevermore" (Ps. 16:11). Knowing that we are constantly in God's presence is a cause for celebration. Psalm 100:1-2 says, "Make a joyful shout to the LORD, all you lands! Serve the LORD with gladness; come before His presence with singing." We can never leave the general presence of God, but we can leave His intimate presence. The psalmist asks us to joyfully come out of the world and from the general presence of God into His intimate presence by worship and praise.

Think again of the life of Jacob. Those few times he did not struggle with selfishness were when he found himself awestruck by God's presence. The presence of God is a source of joy and celebration, but it's also a cause for solemn reverence. One of my favorite children's stories is *The Wind in the Willows*, by Kenneth Grahame. In this delightful story the author depicts two creatures in the commanding presence of the Piper. "'Rat,' the mole found breath to whisper, shaking, 'Are you afraid?' 'Afraid?' murmured the rat, his eyes shinning with unutterable love. 'Afraid, of Him? Oh, never, never. And yet, and yet, O Mole, I am afraid.' And, crouching to the earth, they bowed their heads."[2] While Grahame was not describing God in his story, this is a beautiful description of how we should behave ourselves in the commanding presence of the God of all gods.

There is no room for selfishness in the intimate presence of God. Selfishness may offer a tip of the hat, but never true reverence. It is an indication of the selfishness of our day that we no longer have a true reverence, let alone a fear, in God's presence. Dr. Ed Young observed, "Today we have replaced true reverence for God with something much smaller and more manageable—respect."[3] Respect is no match for reverence. We must respect God, but that's not enough when you recognize in whose presence you crouch.

Unselfish responses

God expects far more than respect. He demands an unselfish reverence—a reverence that calls for appropriate responses.

Because of his tricky behavior, Jacob was forced to flee from Esau. On his way to stay with his uncle Laban, his mother's brother, he camped overnight in the wilderness.

During the night Jacob had a vision in the form of a dream in which God revealed His special plans for him.

When Jacob woke from his sleep, he didn't simply respect God; he absolutely feared God. He said, "How awesome is this place" (Gen. 28:17). He followed this observation with actions that proved he had a genuine reverence for God. How will you know when you do more than merely respect God? How will you know when you have an awesome fear of God as both friend and Creator? A true reverence for God will result in:

An immediate response

Jacob "rose early in the morning" (v. 18). He didn't get a committee together. He didn't find out what the others thought he should do. He knew that he had to respond to God. His response had to be decisive and immediate. He couldn't wait; he rose early in the morning and got busy responding to the awesome presence of God.

When God moves into your life, when your righteous relationship with Him through Jesus Christ opens the door for His intimate presence, your response should be immediate. Historians report that during the American Revolution, Colonel Rahl, commander of the British troops at Trenton, New Jersey, was playing cards when a courier brought an urgent message stating that General George Washington was crossing the Delaware River. Rahl put the letter in his pocket and didn't bother to read it until the game had finished. Then, realizing the seriousness of the situation, he hurriedly tried to rally his men to meet the impending attack, but his procrastination was his undoing. He and many of his men were killed, and the rest of his regiment were captured by

Washington's troops. Only a few minutes delay cost Rahl his life and honor and the liberty of his soldiers.

If God is worthy of our reverence, He is worthy of it *now*. Don't think about showing God your respect and reverence on the weekend. He is God now, not just on Sunday. The God of the universe demands our immediate attention. Give it to Him.

A memorable response

Verse 18 says that Jacob "took the stone that he had put at his head, set it up as a pillar, and poured oil on top of it." The word translated "pillar" is *matstsebah*. It means something that is stationary, a memorial stone. It was not an altar used for sacrifice but a column used as a reminder. Jacob established memorial stones on several occasions. He erected a pillar here at Bethel (28:18), one at Mizpah (31:45-51), another at Bethel (35:14) and one on the way to Ephrath (Bethlehem, 35:19-20), where Rachel died. Jacob had experiences at these sites that he did not want to forget.

The first pillar at Bethel was a reminder of an incredible oversight. God had been there, and Jacob had failed to realize it until after He had gone. Most of us have some pillars in our lives that are reminders of some incredible oversights. Perhaps it was a letter that should have been written or a visit put off until too late. And we say, "I'll not do that again!" So we erect pillars. Oh, they're not actual stone pillars, as Jacob's were, but they are mental reminders. The problem is that time erases those mental reminders and thus the vitality and longevity of our responses.

Perhaps we should convert some of those mental reminders into physical ones. I have found that I benefit from such physical reminders. That's why every believer should as often as possible participate in the Lord's Supper. The elements of the bread and cup remind us afresh of Christ's sacrificial love for us, of His broken body and spilled blood, and of our responsibility to remain faithful to Him "till He comes" (1 Cor. 11:26).

It is so easy to forget even important events and people. Speaking of America, the fractured country he served as 16th president, Abraham Lincoln said, "We have been the recipients of the choicest bounties of heaven. We have grown in numbers, wealth, and power, as no other nation has ever grown. But we have forgotten God." Perhaps we Americans, and all Christians, need to erect some memorial stones to aid us in remaining faithful to God—a date and note in the flyleaf of our Bible, a special place for our devotions, a Scripture verse on the wall—to jog our memory of what Christ has done for us. As the old Chinese proverb says, "The weakest ink is stronger than the strongest memory." Erect some meaningful pillars along your spiritual pilgrimage with the Lord. They will help anchor you to the right pathway.

A *life-changing response*

Jacob made a vow that would affect the rest of his life. He said, "If God will be with me, and keep me in this way that I am going, and give me bread to eat and clothing to put on, so that I come back to my father's house in peace, then the LORD shall be my God. And this stone which I have set as a pillar shall be God's house, and of all that You give me I will surely give a tenth to You" (Gen. 28:20-22).

Even though Jacob missed God's presence, he still claimed God's promise. Furthermore, he cemented that claim with a vow. Vows are more than promises; they are verbal contracts with God. It may be true as someone claimed that "vows made in storms are forgotten in calm," but it wasn't true of Jacob. He believed as Solomon did, "When you make a vow to God, do not delay to pay it; for He has no pleasure in fools. Pay what you have vowed" (Eccl. 5:4). And Jacob did.

What's the only proper response to the presence of God? A response that positively affects every area of your life. When we enter into the intimate presence of God, even though we have been selfish, the question of giving to God will be a non-issue. Those who know the intimate presence of their Lord hold no claim to their possessions, their time or even their physical bodies. These all belong to the One in whose commanding presence we bow.

Missing God's presence

As I understand Scripture, it is impossible for a person to evade the actual presence of God; but it is very possible to lose the intimate presence of God. Jacob's first encounter with God took place while he was fleeing to Haran, and his response was, "Surely the LORD is in this place, and I *did not know it*" (Gen. 28:16, emphasis mine).

Many Christians know that God is everywhere. If asked, they would agree that God is present wherever they are in the world. But in their hectic concern for earning a living, raising a family and paying off the mortgage, they have slowly lost the intimate presence of God in their lives—and worse yet, may not even know it. Selfishness puts us to sleep, and while we slumber we silently, imperceptibly drift from the intimacy of God's presence.

Samson ripped apart a lion, killed 1,000 men with the jawbone of an ass, carried off the gates of Gaza and did many other amazing feats because the Lord was with him. Delilah, however, wormed the secret of his strength from him and sheared his hair while he slept. Then she called out, "The Philistines are upon you, Samson!" So he woke up and said, "I will go out as before, at other times, and shake myself free!" But one of the saddest verse in the Bible continues, "he did not know that the LORD had departed from him" (Judges 16:20). What a tragedy! Samson was so caught up in getting his own selfish desires met that he never noticed that he had slipped out of the meaningful presence of the Lord.

There is nothing more sorrowful than discovering you have strayed away from God's intimate presence. Although hell is a real place of future torment and not just a hell on earth, as some folks say, there are a lot of people who are living a hellish existence because they have foolishly wandered away from the intimate presence of God.

For those who have not received Jesus Christ as Savior, there is an even more dreadful future awaiting them than just the absence of God's intimate presence today. Jesus predicted, "And then I will declare to them, 'I never knew you; depart from Me, you who practice lawlessness!'" (Matt. 7:23). The apostle Paul described their fate even more graphically:

> When the Lord Jesus is revealed from heaven with His mighty angels, in flaming fire taking vengeance on those who do not know God, and on those who do not obey the gospel of our Lord Jesus Christ. These shall be punished with everlasting destruction from the presence of the Lord and from the glory of His power, when He comes, in that Day (2 Thess. 1:7-10).

For all eternity they will be cut off from the very thing they were created for and that which brings the most joy—the intimate presence of God. The greatest torment of hell is the absence of God!

When Jacob awakened from his sleep, he realized, "God was here and I didn't know it." Don't let this happen to you. As one who has been cleansed by the blood of Jesus Christ, you have a righteousness that allows you to experience the intimate presence of God—if you don't let Satan lull you to sleep.

If you have not received Christ, you still have time. Before the terrible day when Jesus will say, "Depart from me, I never knew you," you can ask Him to be your Savior and remove you from the horrors of hell to the eternal presence of God in heaven. Believe that Jesus died to pay the penalty for your sin. Admit that without Him you are lost and on your way to an eternity without God. And then in faith trust that Jesus will save you if you ask Him and place His righteousness around you, giving you new life, a new destiny and a new opportunity to enjoy being reconnected with God forever. Only Jesus Christ can make it possible for you to be declared righteous and experience the joy of God's intimate presence.

1 David Seamands, *Healing for Damaged Emotions* (Wheaton, Ill.: Victor Books, 1984), p. 130.

2 Kenneth Grahame, *The Wind in the Willows* (New York: Barnes & Noble, 1995), p. 182.

3 Ed Young, "Reverence," *Moody*, September 1995, p. 16.

Chapter 4

CHOOSING THE SOLITARY WAY

———— ✍ ————

Six weeks before he died, Elvis Presley was asked by a reporter, "Elvis, when you started playing music, you said you wanted three things in life: you wanted to be rich, you wanted to be famous, and you wanted to be happy. Are you happy?" Elvis replied, "No. I'm as lonely as anyone could be."

Unfortunately, a great many people could say the same thing today. One of the tragedies of our society is how lonely people really are. There's a lot being written these days about loneliness. Psychologist Eric Fromm says, "We have developed a phobia about being alone. We prefer the most trivial and obnoxious company, the most meaningless activity to being alone. We seem to be frightened of the prospect of facing ourselves. Because people don't want to be alone, they will search out others even if they don't like the people they search out. They'll go to activities even if they don't enjoy the activities simply because of our phobia of being alone." Is it possible Fromm is right? Albert Einstein probably would have agreed. He once said, "It's a strange thing to be so well known and yet be so alone." Mr. Einstein was not all alone, but he was a very lonely man.

In Genesis 32 we find Jacob all alone. As he started back home and got ready to cross over to the Promised Land, he received the news that his brother, Esau, was coming with 400 men. For the first time in 20 years, Jacob was about to encounter his brother. How would

Esau react? Was it possible he had forgotten his anger? Jacob didn't know, but he wasn't taking any chances. He lined up his wives and children, his cows and camels and all the other livestock. Hoping to appease his brother—or at least soften his wrath—Jacob sent the women, children, all the servants and the animals on before him.

Then something unique happened in the life of Jacob. Genesis 32:24 says, "And Jacob was left alone. " This is the first time in the story of Jacob that the writer makes it a point to tell us that Jacob was all alone. Up until now, except for the journey from his father's home in Canaan to his Uncle Laban's home in Haran, he had been with people all the time. But not now. Suddenly, Jacob was experiencing the sensation of being alone.

There are many people who find themselves alone. Some are widows or widowers. Some are single adults who live by themselves. Others are single parents and they, too, are alone, devoid of adult companionship. University students constitute yet another group that often suffers in solitude. Many teenagers feel alone and think no one understands them. Being alone is a common experience.

But the Bible makes a clear distinction between being alone and experiencing loneliness versus being alone and experiencing solitude. When you choose to walk away from your selfish attitudes of the past, you may find yourself alone. God's plan, however, is that you experience solitude, not loneliness. Loneliness brings danger; solitude brings blessings.

The dangers of loneliness

What are some of the dangers that lonely people face? If you are living in loneliness today, what devastating effects can a lonely life bring to you? Let's investigate.

Loneliness can disorientate

Have you ever visited a far-off place and stayed in a motel? Did you awaken in the middle of the night a bit disoriented? Maybe you stumbled into the closet instead of into the bathroom. Because your surroundings were unfamiliar, perhaps for a few moments you didn't have a clue where you were. I do a lot of traveling, so sometimes I will wake in a strange place and wonder, *Where am I? What country am I in? Where is this place?* I've decided not to start worrying until I begin to wonder, *Who am I?* Becoming disoriented happens when you're alone.

When we're disoriented, there's the danger of making a wrong decision. In the confusion of the moment, we can easily take a wrong turn, go the wrong way or get so confused we end up going nowhere. Right after Linda and I were married we packed everything we owned in the back seat of a 1959 Nash Rambler and headed off to a tiny apartment in a distant state. I was continuing my education, and we rented two rooms upstairs from an elderly woman who was hard of hearing. She had the telephone company replace the old bells on her phone with two four-inch bells so when the phone rang she could hear it. The first night we lived with her the phone rang. Both Linda and I sprang from the bed—I to the hallway to answer the phone, and she to a nearby wall. When I returned I found her half-dazed, disoriented and scratching the wall mumbling, "Where is that door? It was right here."

The disorientation that often accompanies loneliness has influenced people to make decisions they would never have made in better moments. The president of a Christian college lost his wife quite suddenly from a brain aneurism. In the following months he struggled with loneliness and grief. In the midst of these stressful events, he chose to quickly marry a woman who had been divorced several times. The ensuing debate over the biblical appropriateness of this relationship cost him the presidency of that college.

Lonely people are vulnerable. In the throes of their loneliness, they are open to decisions and situations that they may later regret. They lose perspective on what they ought to do. Selfishly, they think only of the pain of their loneliness and forget that other people's lives will be impacted by their choices. Loneliness is the wrong basis for making a decision.

Loneliness can turn us inward

When we're alone our lives also tend to turn inward. When that happens, we can become self-absorbed and our selfishness grows. We become aware of all our aches and pains. We brood on the unfairness and injustices of life. We stew over real and sometimes imagined offenses. The resulting bitterness and sour attitude cause even greater loneliness.

I read that a couple named Jim and Linda Onan of Wadsworth, Illinois, wanted an unusual house. Accordingly, they built a 7,000-square-foot pyramid covered in 24-karat gold. The house is surrounded by a moat, which the Onans plan to stock with sharks.

Lonely people frequently build similar habitats covered with selfishness. They fill their moat with the sharks of resentfulness and complaint. They invite no one in and make it clear that they want to keep everyone out. Then they wonder why no one comes to visit.

Loneliness can actually be a dietary aid to selfishness. It can feed our self-centeredness until we become even more selfish. That's why it's difficult—in fact, deadly—when we're alone and self-absorbed. But it's possible to be alone and not be lonely. It's possible to be in solitude and yet not be alone. Let me explain.

The blessings of solitude

The alternative to being alone and selfish is being alone and blessed. The Bible says that even if you are alone, you can enjoy and appreciate that. You can enjoy and appreciate solitude. The philosopher Paul Tillich said, "Language has created the word *loneliness* to express the pain of being alone, and the word *solitude* to express the glory of being alone." Being in solitude provides opportunities that can be found nowhere else.

The opportunity for self-evaluation

As Jacob sat alone waiting to literally wrestle with God, he came to realize how empty and needy he was. As long as he had the distraction of family and friends, the comforts of wealth and possessions, he could fool himself into believing that he was self-sufficient and in need of nothing. He was like the church at Laodicea, which

47

claimed, "I am rich, have become wealthy, and have need of nothing"; but Jesus said they did not know they were "wretched, miserable, poor, blind, and naked" (Rev. 3:17). The solution? Jesus said, "I counsel you to buy from Me gold refined in the fire, that you may be rich; and white garments, that you may be clothed, that the shame of your nakedness may not be revealed; and anoint your eyes with eye salve, that you may see" (v. 18).

Jacob didn't have the Book of Revelation to read, but he took that advice anyway. He told the Angel of the Lord, "I will not let You go unless You bless me!" Before being left alone, Jacob had been self-satisfied and independent. He had plenty, with no need for anything from anybody. Now he realized that he needed God's blessing on his life. Have you come to realize that as well?

In a busy, hectic world, Christians desperately need time for solitude in which they can evaluate their lives. They need time alone where they can prayerfully ask, "Search me, O God, and know my heart; try me, and know my anxieties; and see if there is any wicked way in me, and lead me in the way everlasting" (Ps. 139:23-24). Theologian Henri Nouwen said, "In solitude our heart can slowly take off its many protective devices and can grow so wide and deep that nothing human is strange to it. Then we can become contrite, crushed and broken." This kind of heart change will never happen if we don't get alone.

The opportunity for intimacy with God

One of the best things that can ever happen to us is to have the opportunity to spend time alone with God. In his solitude at Peniel, Jacob, who had been selfish all the days of his life, realized for the first time that his loneliness did not have to feed his selfishness. Instead, his loneliness could be a time of learning to appreciate God even more.

Shallowness is the hallmark of our age. We avoid intimacy because it may be inconvenient. We don't want to get closely involved with someone's life because we might have demands placed on us that we aren't willing to meet. Even God is only a nodding acquaintance. The French philosopher Voltaire once described his relationship with Christ by saying, "We salute, but we do not speak." Many people, including Christians, could say the same.

The tragedy of this approach to life is that we never discover the enrichment that other people can bring to us. We never discover the incredible enrichment that God brings to our lives. The psalmist said, "Yea, though I walk through the valley of the shadow of death, I will fear no evil; for You are with me; Your rod and Your staff, they comfort me" (Ps. 23:4). The more we know Christ, the less we fear anything else. Again in the Psalms we find the joyous testimony, "I will be glad and rejoice in You; I will sing praise to Your name, O Most High" (9:2). What comfort and joy is ours when we know God intimately. And solitude, more than any other situation, gives us the opportunity to get to know God intimately.

God's gracious invitation

Psalm 102 is for all people who are alone, for people living in solitude. It brings great joy and comfort when there is no one else around. Here are some selected verses from that psalm.

Hear my prayer, O LORD, and let my cry come to You. Do not hide Your face from me in the day of my trouble; incline Your ear to me; in the day that I call, answer me speedily. For my days are consumed like smoke, and my bones are burned like a hearth. . . . I am like a pelican of the wilderness; I am like an owl of the desert. I lie awake, and am like a sparrow alone on the housetop. My enemies reproach me all day long, and those who deride me swear an oath against me. . . . But You, O LORD, shall endure forever, and the remembrance of Your name to all generations. . . . For the LORD shall build up Zion; He shall appear in His glory. He shall regard the prayer of the destitute, and shall not despise their prayer. . . . Of old You laid the foundation of the earth, and the heavens are the work of Your hands. They will perish, but You will endure; yes, they will all grow old like a garment; like a cloak You will change them, and they will be changed. But You are the same, and Your years will have no end. The children of Your servants will continue, and their descendants will be established before You (vv. 1-3, 6-8, 12, 16-17, 25-28).

Admittedly, the opening verses of this psalm are not very encouraging, but they are a good description of how people who are alone sometimes feel. In verse 7 the psalmist talks about being "like a sparrow on top of the house." What an accurate picture of loneliness this is.

But right in the middle of this psalm, beginning in verse 12, the psalmist, who was alone and decrying the fact that he had to spend his life alone, suddenly changed his view. Loneliness changed to solitude. Loneliness changed to an understanding that in his loneliness he was with God, who has promised, "Do not be afraid, nor be dismayed, for the LORD your God is with you wherever you go" (Josh. 1:9). In the New Testament the writer of Hebrews reminds us, "[God] will never leave you nor forsake you" (13:5). All at once it seems that the psalmist recognized that God was there and His promises were active and real. God was present in the midst of his loneliness and He wanted to have special fellowship with the psalmist. That made all the difference between loneliness and solitude.

Several years ago God changed my prayer habits. I wanted to be empowered to pray, so I would get up each morning around 4:30. I would then spend an hour or so reading the Word and praying to the Lord. I divided that hour equally between reading and praying. But then God impressed upon me that I was missing something in my time with Him. I needed more intimacy, more solitude, more time to do nothing but wait on Him. So now I divide my time into three segments: I spend a third of my time reading and meditating on God's Word, a third of my time talking with Him in prayer and a third of my time doing nothing. I just wait on the Lord—alone, in solitude, musing over the things I have read in his Word, remembering His great promises, letting Him impress upon me the things I need to be impressed with for that day. It's my time to be alone in intimacy with my Heavenly Father. I'm like Jacob waiting to wrestle for the day, all alone but not afraid and not lonely. If you can grasp the difference between being alone and enjoying solitude with God, you'll never be lonely again.

In this world of nearly 6 billion people, it's amazing how lonely people can be. Obviously, our lack of intimacy with other people is only symptomatic of our lack of intimacy with God. Choosing the solitary way is choosing the best way. In the saga of Jacob, one of the secrets of overcoming selfishness was the intimacy of his solitude with God. If you want more intimacy and less selfishness, try the solitary way. This is not a "do-it yourself spirituality"; it's a "let-God-do-it solitude."

Chapter 5

CHOOSING THE HUMBLE WAY

—— 🖋 ——

When Ronald Reagan was president of the United States, he returned to his ancestral home in Ireland. The name of the village that held his roots was Ballyporeen, which means "the town of small potatoes." I can identify with that. I was raised in a small town in Pennsylvania that had only one commercial building—and it served as the train station, the gas station, the post office and the general store.

The truth is, most people are from "the town of small potatoes," but many would hate to admit it. Jacob certainly would have had difficulty confessing such a fact. It's humbling to acknowledge that we're only a "small potato," and humility is something that Jacob, along with many of us, had a difficult time practicing. In fact, we would try just about every other avenue before resorting to humbling ourselves. That's what Jacob did.

When Jacob left the land of Canaan, God appeared to him in a dream. Jacob saw a ladder reaching up to heaven, and at the top of the ladder was the Lord God Himself. God promised Jacob that he would someday return to his homeland (Gen. 28:13-15). When Jacob woke up, he realized that God had been in that place, so he called it Bethel (literally: "house of God").

Jacob traveled on from Bethel and spent the next 20 years matching wits with his uncle Laban. But the day came when the Angel of God appeared to Jacob and said, "I am the God of Bethel, where you anointed the pillar and where you made a vow to Me. Now arise, get out of this land, and return to the land of your kindred" (Gen. 31:13). So Jacob gathered his family together and began his journey back, all the while thinking, *If I go back to the Promised Land, I have to go back to the people I've cheated, swindled and deceived. And worst of all, I have to go back and face my brother, Esau.*

When long-separated relatives get together, it's often a joyous occasion. But this is one reunion that Jacob gladly would have skipped. You might feel the same way if the last time you saw your brother you had cheated him and you knew he hated you. In fact, the last words that Jacob heard from Esau, as reported by his mother, were, "The days of mourning for my father are at hand; then I will kill my brother Jacob" (Gen. 27:41). Twenty years later as he traveled back to his homeland, the first thing Jacob heard from the people he sent ahead as a reconnaissance group was, "By the way, Esau's looking for you too. He has 400 men with him." That's enough to cause anyone concern! And Jacob began again to plot how he might encounter Esau and not be killed. The thought that he could simply humble himself and beg Esau's forgiveness never entered his mind—at least not until every other avenue was exhausted. Rather than admit that he was only a "small potato," Jacob exhausted all the other alternatives first, such as:

Appealing to family ties

In Genesis 32:4, Jacob commanded his messengers to tell Esau, "Thus your servant Jacob says: 'I have sojourned with Laban and stayed there until now.'" Obviously, Esau knew who Laban was. He was as much Esau's uncle as he was Jacob's. But Jacob's subtle hint was, "Hey, Esau, you remember me! I've been spending time with our uncle—you know, Uncle Laban. We have the same uncle. We're brothers! Let's just let bygones be bygones."

Family ties are very important in the Middle East. When I was 19, I visited the Holy Land for the first time. I stopped at a shop in Damascus, Syria, and struck up a conversation with the shopkeeper, who was also 19. In the course of our visit he invited me to come to his house, and I accepted. After he closed the shop we made our way through some alleys and finally came to a door. When my newly made friend opened the door, we went into a lovely, spacious courtyard with palm trees and flowers. Off of this courtyard must have been a dozen or more doors. I asked, "Where do these doors go?" "Well," my friend said, "behind that door lives Uncle Fred, and there's Aunty Lucy," and so on. The names were different, of course, but I came to realize that the whole family lived in that one complex. It was a family house. Father, mother, grandfather, uncles, aunts, nephews, dogs, cats—the whole family lived in that one area.

In the Middle East of biblical times, the emphasis on family was no less important. Genesis 11:31 talks about Abraham's family ties: "And Terah took his son Abram and his grandson Lot, the son of Haran, and his daughter-in-law Sarai, his son Abram's wife, and they went out with them from Ur of the Chaldeans to go to the land of Canaan; and they came to Haran and dwelt there." Everyone defined by their relationship to one another: son, grandson, son, daughter-in-law, wife of a son. A person's significance was directly related to his family connections.

It was only natural, then, that Jacob would first appeal to family ties. But it didn't work. Esau wasn't impressed.

Appealing to wealth

Since family ties weren't making an impression, Jacob decided to impress Esau with his wealth. He said, "I have oxen, donkeys, flocks, and male and female servants; and I have sent to tell my lord, that I may find favor in your sight" (Gen. 32:5). Jacob must have been thinking, *Surely Esau will fall down before me and say, "Oh, there's no problem between you and me. Not a wealthy guy like you."*

Certainly there is nothing wrong with being rich. God's Word records that many of His servants in the Old Testament were wealthy men. Abraham and Lot were so wealthy that they couldn't remain together because there wasn't enough grazing land for their combined herds. They were rich men!

Furthermore, Genesis 23 tells us that when Abraham approached Ephron, the son of Zohar, to buy the cave of Machpelah in which to bury his wife, Sarah, Ephron said, "My lord, hear me; the land is worth four hundred shekels of silver. What is that between you and me?" (Gen. 23:15). Between you and me that would probably be a lot, but between these two guys, it wasn't anything. They were so wealthy that 400 shekels of silver was just pocket change.

Scripture also mentions other rich men. Solomon was not only the wisest man of his day, he was also the richest. In his latter days, Job was said to possess 14,000 sheep, 6,000 camels, 1,000 yoke of oxen and 1,000 female donkeys. That was a tidy sum of four-footed wealth. In the New Testament, Joseph of Aramethia was a wealthy man who gave his tomb for Jesus' burial, and

Nicodemus was a wealthy Jew who came to Jesus at night and later became a believer.

There's nothing wrong with wealth as long as the way we get it and the way we use it pleases God. But Jacob's fault was that he displayed his wealth to try to impress and manipulate his brother.

Yet that didn't work either. Esau was no pauper. When Abraham set out to rescue his nephew Lot (Gen. 14:12-16), he took with him 318 trained servants who were part of his household. In other words, Abraham had a private army of more than 300 warriors. But when Esau came to meet Jacob, he had an army of 400 warriors. Esau was rich himself, so Jacob didn't impress him with how much he had.

Appealing to flattering words

When all else failed, Jacob attempted to wheedle his way around Esau with flattering words. In Genesis 32:17-18, Jacob told his servants, "When Esau my brother meets you and asks you, saying, 'To whom do you belong, and where are you going? Whose are these in front of you?' then you shall say, 'They are your servant Jacob's. It is a present sent to my lord Esau; and behold, he also is behind us.'"

This doesn't sound much like the way brothers talk to each other. A more common relationship is described by one mother who says, "My children don't merely argue. Instead, they frequently engage in ritualized exercises in terrorism—hand-to-hand, or soccer shoe-to-shin combat, as the case may be. [Having three children] is sometimes like having members of three rival gangs living under one roof: The Whiners, The Teasers and

The I'm-Almost-a-Teenager-and-Everyone-Else-Is-a-Nerd clubs, each with a membership of one."[1] This description adds an air of believability to the story of the Sunday school teacher who asked if any of the Ten Commandments applied to brothers and sisters. One young boy piped up with the suggestion, "Thou shalt not kill."

But Jacob was on his best behavior as he contemplated Esau's approach. Honey would hardly have melted in his mouth. He called Esau "lord." The Hebrew word used here is *'adown*, which means "sovereign, master or owner." That word in the plural (*adonai*) is applied 450 times with reference to God in the King James Version. As Floyd Barackman notes, "This title expresses a personal relationship—one of authority on the one hand, and of allegiance and love on the other."[2] Having called Esau "lord," Jacob called himself a bondservant (*'ebed*), one who is in total subjection to another. This was not done in true humility, however; it was more on the order of groveling. Often when selfishness is trying to hide itself under a guise of humbleness, it goes to the extreme. This was the case with Jacob. He didn't truly believe what he said; it was a formality. Since nothing else had worked, he was willing to stoop to flattery if it served his purpose. As the philosopher Aesop pointed out, "Men seldom flatter without a purpose; and they who listen to such music may expect to pay the piper."

Kind words, of course, are not wrong. Peter urged us to put on brotherly kindness (2 Pet. 1:7). Kindness is listed as a fruit of the Spirit (Gal. 5:22). Paul exhorted the Christians at Ephesus to "be kind to one another, tenderhearted, forgiving one another, just as God in Christ forgave you" (4:32). But kind words are sincere. They are meant to point out genuine merit and appreciation. That was not the case with Jacob. His kindness was just another way of expressing his selfishness.

What really works

Jacob tried to gain forgiveness by appealing to family relationships. He got no answer. He attempted to appeal to wealth and Esau replied, "I have enough, my brother; keep what you have for yourself" (Gen. 33:9). Jacob sought to flatter and it had no effect.

So what was left? Humility. Genesis 33:4 says, "But Esau ran to meet him, and embraced him, and fell on his neck and kissed him, and they wept." These were not simply tears of long-separated relatives; they were tears of confession and forgiveness. Tears washed away the years of bitterness and resentment and softened a selfish heart. They were possibly the first sincere thing that Jacob and Esau ever had done together.

The late Vance Havner liked to relate the story of an elderly lady who was greatly disturbed by her many troubles, both real and imaginary. Finally her family told her kindly, "Grandma, we've done all we can do for you. You'll just have to trust God for the rest." A look of utter despair spread over her face as she replied, "Oh, dear, has it come to that?" Havner noted that it always comes to that.

When we want forgiveness and restoration, we can try many things. We can manipulate and scheme; we can try to bribe and cajole. But ultimately it will come down to humility. When we humble ourselves, we usually find a gracious reception. David said, "The sacrifices of God are a broken spirit, a broken and a contrite heart—these, O God, You will not despise" (Ps. 51:17).

Is there someone in your life you need to come home to? Someone you have been estranged from for a long time? Forget your plans and schemes. Just go to him or her in humility and tears. God will do the rest.

---

1 Cindy Lange-Kubick, "Children—studies in domestic terrorism," *Lincoln Journal Star*, August 21, 1995.

2 Floyd Hays Barackman, *Practical Christian Theology* (Grand Rapids, Mich.: Kregel Publications, 1992), p. 54.

Chapter 6

CHOOSING THE WORSHIPFUL WAY

———— ✒ ————

Selfishness is all about finding satisfaction in life. Certainly there is nothing wrong with that goal. It's how we attain satisfaction that can be the evidence of selfishness.

Genesis describes Abraham's death this way: "Then Abraham breathed his last and died in a good old age, an old man and full of years, and was gathered to his people" (Gen. 25:8). Here is a man who reached his latter years and could say, "I'm satisfied." The same is true for Simeon in the Gospel of Luke. When Mary and Joseph brought Jesus to the temple to be dedicated, Simeon at once recognized that this was no ordinary baby; this was the promised Messiah. His response was, "Lord, now You are letting Your servant depart in peace, according to Your word; for my eyes have seen Your salvation which You have prepared before the face of all peoples, a light to bring revelation to the Gentiles, and the glory of Your people Israel" (Luke 2:29-32). Again, here is a man who came to the end of his years with great satisfaction.

The problem with pursuing satisfaction is not the goal—it's the method. Satan has sold the human race a bill of goods. He says, "Satisfaction is found by putting yourself first. Only if you're looking out for your own needs can you be guaranteed a satisfied life." God wants us to live a satisfied life as well. But He knows it can't be done the way Satan suggests. Putting yourself at the center of your existence, selfishly seeking to make your desires the most important thing in your life, will never leave you satisfied. Satisfaction comes not as you focus on yourself but as you focus on God. That is the primary purpose of worship.

Either selfishness will keep us from true worship, or worship will keep us from total selfishness. Both of these truths were at work in Jacob's life.

Conditional worship

The first time we see Jacob worshiping is when he fled for his life to his Uncle Laban's home in Haran. As he camped overnight on the way, he dreamed that God appeared to him and assured him that not only would He keep him safe, He would bring him back home as well.

Jacob's response was one of overwhelming awe and fear. When he awoke from his sleep he said, "Surely the LORD is in this place, and I did not know it." And he was afraid and said, "How awesome is this place! This is none other than the house of God, and this is the gate of heaven!" (Gen. 28:16-17). Jacob's heart must have been pounding. A cold sweat likely broke out on his forehead. He stood in awe.

Man's response to a genuine encounter with God is one of reverence. Dr. Ed Young, well-known pastor and author, notes, "Reverence is the only appropriate response to God. If we do not revere Him, it is because we have not seen Him as He truly is. It is impossible to behold God in His majesty, mercy, and mystery, and not experience an unbidden holy fear."[1] But this isn't worship. Worship is our response to this experience of awe and fear.

What was Jacob's response? Selfishness took over and he began to bargain with God. He said, "If God will be with me, and keep me in this way that I am going, and give me bread to eat and clothing to put on, so that I come back to my father's house in peace, then the LORD shall be my God. And this stone which I have set as a pillar shall be God's house, and of all that You give me I will surely give a tenth to You" (Gen. 28:20-22).

Jacob put conditions on his worship. In effect he said, "God, if you treat me right, if you uphold your end of the contract and keep me, give me bread and clothing and bring me back home, THEN I will worship you and give you ten percent of my possessions." Jacob wasn't about to worship God without the assurance he was going to get something in return.

What does bargaining with God say to you? It implies that He has needs that we can meet in return for His help in achieving the things we want. But the Bible says that God has no needs. When Paul preached to the men of Athens at the Areopagus, he declared, "Nor is He [God] worshiped with men's hands, as though He needed anything, since He gives to all life, breath, and all things" (Acts 17:25). God is not a used car salesman. He has no reason to make deals. Though God often chooses to give generously, it is always by His grace, not in any way to have His needs met by us.

Much of what passes for worship today is a thinly disguised bargaining session. "God, I will come to Your house on Sunday, sing hymns and try to stay awake during the sermon. I will even give You a portion of my possessions. In return I expect You to bless me the other six days of the week. If You don't bless me, I'll stop attending, and then who will worship You?" That kind of

63

haggling might be appropriate for the marketplace, but it's certainly not appropriate for the worship place. God will have no negotiated worship.

Worship is owed, not earned. God doesn't have to do anything to be worthy of worship; our worship is due Him because He is God. We don't have a single bargaining chip with which to wheel and deal with God. He has no needs that we can meet and no binding commitments we can manipulate. God is God, and that fact alone requires our worship.

True worship

For the next 20 years Jacob muddled along with his mistaken concept of worship. His relationship with God revolved around his needs and desires. Relying on his own cunning, he conducted a battle of wits with his uncle, Laban, until finally the tide turned. Jacob grew prosperous while Laban became a has-been. But this didn't bring Jacob the peace and joy he thought it would. Instead, Laban's sons, Jacob's brothers-in-law, grew to hate him. Jacob discovered once again that his selfishness gained him more enemies than friends. It was then that God appeared again in a dream and instructed Jacob to return to his homeland.

This was the beginning of a slide into crisis. Jacob's secure little world, a world he had carved out with his own craftiness, began to crumble. First he was pursued and overtaken by Laban. Without God's intervention he would have been killed and all his hard-earned possessions taken back to Haran. It was only God's warning in a dream to Laban that spared Jacob from a tragic ending to his life (Gen. 31:24-29).

Then he had to face Esau. A brother he had manipulated and cheated two decades earlier was on his way with a band of 400 soldiers. Was Jacob scared? Wouldn't you be scared? All his years of selfish living had not prepared him for the grim possibilities he now faced. His finely honed deviousness couldn't help him find a way out of the hole he had been digging for himself over the last 20 years. Nothing he tried seemed to have any effect on his brother. Jacob couldn't run, he couldn't hide, he couldn't manipulate his way out of this one. He had to face his brother. It was then, for the first time, Jacob took the initiative and genuinely sought the Lord.

Alone at a place called Peniel, he wrestled with the Angel of the Lord until he couldn't wrestle anymore. There was only one thing left to do—cling. Jacob finally came to the end of himself. He realized his own emptiness and cried out to the Angel, "I will not let You go unless You bless me!" For the first time he was making a request not out of greedy selfishness but out of desperate need. There was no bargaining. God could fill that need any way He chose, but Jacob had seen God through new eyes. He knew that only God could fill the emptiness he felt on the inside. Jacob realized he could never truly be filled unless God chose to fill him.

So often we go to church so full of ourselves there's no room for God. We've been so busy during the week that we aren't even aware of how empty and needy we are. We fail to appreciate the awesomeness of the One we supposedly came to worship. It makes you wonder if we really believe all the claims we make about God.

John Piper observes: "Scientists know that light travels at the speed of 5.87 trillion miles in a year. They also know that the galaxy of which our solar system is a part is about 100,000 light-years in diameter—about 587,000 trillion miles. It is one of about a million such galaxies in the optical range of our most powerful telescopes. In our galaxy there are about 100 billion stars. The sun is one of them, a modest star burning at about 6,000 degrees centigrade on the surface, and traveling in an orbit at 155 miles per second, which means it will take about 200 million years to complete a revolution around the galaxy.

"Scientists who know these things are awed by them. And they say, 'If there is a personal God, as the Christians say, who spoke this universe into being, then there is a certain respect and reverence and wonder and dread that would have to come through when they talk about Him and when they worship Him.'"[2] Well, this personal God does exist, but these attitudes are frequently lacking because of our self-centeredness. Worship is viewed as an opportunity to feel good about ourselves rather than worship the Person and character of God. We come ready to bargain with God rather than surrender. Yet it's only when we are willing to let go of ourselves that true worship can begin.

Lasting change

For the first time in his life Jacob had a true worship experience, and he went away a changed man. Genesis 32:25 records, "Now when He [the Angel of the Lord] saw that He did not prevail against him, He touched the socket of his hip; and the socket of Jacob's hip was out of joint as He wrestled with him." Richard Foster was right when he wrote, "If worship does not change us, it has not been worship. To stand before the Holy One of eternity is to change. . . . Just as worship begins in holy expectancy, it ends in holy obedience."[3]

Back when Merv Griffin was hosting his talk show, he interviewed Charlton Heston, the actor who played the part of Moses in *The Ten Commandments* and also starred in the movie *Ben Hur*. Griffin asked Heston if any of the characters he had portrayed in his religious movies had changed his spiritual outlook. Heston didn't answer the question directly. He thought a moment and then simply said, "Well, Merv, you can't walk barefoot down Mount Sinai and be the same person you were when you went up."[4] The same is true for worship. If you leave the worship service at your church no differently than when you went in, you haven't worshiped at all.

Furthermore, true worship leaves a lasting change. Genesis 32:31 says, "Just as he crossed over Peniel the sun rose on him, and he limped on his hip." It is implied that for the rest of his life Jacob limped. God had given him a permanent reminder of his worship experience. As I have observed young people over the years, I've seen them return from summer camp, vacation Bible school or a missions trip and they've been so excited. But within a matter of weeks, life gets back to normal and their interests wane. Adults do the same. Perhaps they attend a series of meetings, become involved in a small group or hear a motivational speaker. For days, weeks or months, they feel their lives are changed. But sooner or later their enthusiasm wears thin and their old lifestyle habits return. But true worship isn't like that. True worship leaves lasting results. True worship changes us forever.

Accepting the change

The change element in worship may be one of the reasons we don't truly seek it. In a study reported by *Leadership* magazine, only 42 percent of the respondents indicated they would be willing to change a bad habit if given the opportunity.[5]

Many people are attracted by the excitement generated at some worship services that encourage more demonstrative forms of worship. But if they were actually confronted with the opportunity to change dramatically, many of them would hesitate. Deep down they feel that if any change is needed, the "other guy" needs it more than they do. "If my wife would change or my husband would change, then I'd be OK. They're the one who really needs it." Selfishly we want everyone and everything to change to fit us without the inconvenience of having to change ourselves and our ways.

Worship, however, never changes the other person; it changes only you. When we choose the worshipful way, we choose the way of change. Paul Rees concludes, "If you can leave your church on Sunday morning with no feeling of discomfort, of conviction, of brokenness, of challenge, then for you the hour of worship has not been as dangerous as it should have been. The ease with which we go on being Christian sentimentalists is one of our worst faults."

No longer can we selfishly focus on ourselves; our focus is on God. When we focus on God, our lives will change and we'll never be the same again. If you could ask Jacob about the changing power of worship, you know what he would say. When we choose the worshipful way, we choose the way of change.

1 Ed Young, "Reverence," *Moody*, September 1995, p. 16.

2 John Piper, "The supremacy of God in missions through worship," *Mission Frontiers*, May-August 1996 *Bulletin of the U.S. Center for World Missions*, Vol. 18, p. 10.

3 Richard J. Foster, *Celebration of Discipline* (San Francisco: Harper & Row, Publishers, 1978), p. 148.

4 David A. Seamands, *God's Blueprint for Living* (Wilmore, Kentucky: Bristol Books, 1988), p. 24.

5 *Leadership*, Winter 1992, Vol. 13, No. 1, p. 79.

Chapter 7

CHOOSING THE WINNING WAY

None of us likes to fail, but failure is a part of life. So is success. If we fail more often than we succeed, we may give in to discouragement. There's always the temptation to throw in the towel and quit. But the benefits of hanging in there just a little longer are significant.

One man who failed often was Thomas Edison. We don't ordinarily think of Edison as a failure because he invented, among other things, the incandescent light bulb. But he failed no less than 14,000 times before he succeeded. Babe Ruth struck out more than any other player in baseball history. But we remember the "Sultan of Swat" for his success as a home run hitter. Failure doesn't mean we can't be a winner.

Even after his experience at Peniel, Jacob failed many times. Selfishness slammed him to the ground time after time, but somehow he always got back up and found his solace in God. As a consequence we don't think of Jacob as a failure. Once he came to know God in a personal way, he stepped into the winner's circle and most of his failures were forgotten. Future generations would come to know God as the "God of Abraham, Isaac and *Jacob*"[1] (Acts 3:13, emphasis mine).

Jacob was a winner, but not because of his own efforts. In his own strength, Jacob was a loser. Yet God met him in his failures and in divine strength made him a winner. Nor is Jacob alone in this experience. God took Rahab, a prostitute, Ruth, a pagan Moabitess, and

Bathsheba, an adulteress, and made them a part of the lineage of Christ—all failures who became winners. He took Moses, a murderer, and made him the leader of Israel. He took the bigoted and violent pharisee Saul and made him the apostle Paul. He took John, a Son of Thunder, and made him the Apostle of Love. All failures who became winners.

Think about it. If God couldn't work with failures, He'd have no one to work with. We are all failures in pleasing God. But God is a pro at making failures into winners. He does that by:

Giving a new nature

Until about 1100 A.D. most people in Europe and elsewhere had only one name. With an ever-growing population, however, came the need to distinguish between people who had common first names. Therefore, people began attaching a surname that came perhaps from an occupation (Cook, Miller), location (Overhill, Brook), ancestors (John's son became Johnson) or personal characteristic (Small, Short, Longfellow).

In biblical times a name was even more than a means of distinguishing one person from another; often a name also reflected a person's character. Nabal (meaning "a stupid, foolish person") in 1 Samuel 25 was certainly true to his name. In the Book of Acts, Barnabas (Son of Encouragement) was a source of encouragement to new believers (Saul in 9:27, new Christians at Antioch in 11:22-24), failures (Mark in 15:37-39) and the church in general (4:36-37).

Jacob's name also reflected his character. Jacob means "supplanter" or "cheater." It comes from the Hebrew word *aw-kab´*,[2] which means to "seize by the heel."[3] And Jacob lived according to his name. He supplanted (or took the place of) his brother Esau in the birthright (Gen. 25:30-34) and cheated him out of his blessing (chp. 27).

But Jacob's wrestling match at Peniel left him a changed man. Even though occasionally he continued to fail by falling back into his old habits, Jacob would never again be a failure. While he never ceased to struggle with selfishness, in the end he was a winner.

To reflect his new character, God gave him a new name. Just as Abram (father) was changed to Abraham (father of a multitude) and Sarai (princess) to Sarah (God's princess), Jacob (cheater, supplanter) was changed to Israel (one who has power [i.e., a prince] with God). Names were not changed lightly in biblical times. It wasn't that Abram liked the name Abraham better. Rather, when Abram believed God would actually make him the father of a multitude (even though his wife hadn't yet borne one son, let alone a multitude), God changed his name to Abraham. When Sarai submitted her skepticism to God's promise and believed that she would bear a son in her old age, God changed her name to Sarah. And when Jacob surrendered his stubborn selfishness to the will of God he, too, received a new character and a new name.

Being a winner is not based on what we do; it's based on who we are. God doesn't simply change our actions; He changes our character. When our character is changed, our actions will follow.

God also has a new name for you and me. When we receive Christ as our Savior, we have a change of character. That doesn't mean we're sinless, nor does it mean we're perfect. It means we're forgiven. We have the presence of God's Holy Spirit in our life. We may fail and fall back temporarily into old patterns of behavior, but God's Spirit won't let us stay there. God is at work on our character. Actions, thoughts and attitudes that never bothered us before now cause us a great deal of discomfort. We have increased sensitivity to those things that the Bible calls sin. That's not just a coincidence; it's the result of a new character. We have a new nature, and that new nature is reflected in a new name. Jesus says, "To him who overcomes I will give . . . a white stone, and on the stone a new name written which no one knows except him who receives it" (Rev. 2:17).

A new character and a new name are part of being in the winner's circle. But they're not all. There's also:

A new confidence

Jacob limped away from his match with the Angel of the Lord with a new confidence. He boldly said to the Angel, "Tell me Your name, I pray." And the Angel said, "Why is it that you ask about My name?" And He blessed Jacob there (Gen. 32:29).

In essence, the Angel was politely saying, "I'm not going to tell you my name." It's not that God enjoys being secretive; but since a name reflected character and God's character is unfathomable, Jacob couldn't have comprehended the name even if the Angel had revealed it. As a result, the name remained unspoken.

Sometimes young children ask questions the answers to which go beyond their understanding (and sometimes beyond our explaining). "Does God have a wife?" "If God doesn't have a wife, how can He have a Son?" As a parent, how will you answer such questions accurately? It's simple. All you must do is explain the nature of the Trinity to a child—not an easy task for even the most experienced parent!

But the important point here is that Jacob had the courage to ask the Angel's name. Jacob had a brand-new confidence. He had survived his all-night wrestling match with the Lord. He didn't win, but he didn't lose either. He had a new name that reflected a new "power with God" (Israel) and Jacob boldly used that new power. He fearlessly asked, "What is your name?"

If you are a Christian you have a new name. Do you also have a new confidence? Hebrews 4:16 says, "Let us therefore come *boldly* to the throne of grace, that we may obtain mercy and find grace to help in time of need" (emphasis mine). We needn't be shrinking violets when it comes to talking with God. Jesus said, "Ask, and it will be given to you; seek, and you will find; knock, and it will be opened to you. For everyone who asks receives, and he who seeks finds, and to him who knocks it will be opened" (Matt. 7:7-8). That's confidence!

When you come to God, do so with the new-found confidence of your new character in Christ. James said, "But let him ask in faith, with no doubting, for he who doubts is like a wave of the sea driven and tossed by the wind. For let not that man suppose that he will receive anything from the Lord; he is a double-minded man, unstable in all his ways" (James 1:6-8). Real faith, genuine faith, is not timid faith. It exudes confidence in God.

Carl Wallenda was one of the greatest tightrope aerialists who ever lived. He wrote, "For me, to live is being on a tightrope. All the rest is waiting." In 1968 he commented that the most important thing about walking a tightrope is to be confident you can do it and never to think about failure. Ten years later, Wallenda fell to his death from a tightrope that was 75 feet up in the air in San Juan, Puerto Rico. His wife, who was also an aerialist, reported that for three months prior to attempting the most dangerous feat he'd ever tried, all Wallenda talked about was falling. She said that never before in all their career together had her husband ever given a thought to falling. She noted further that he spent all of his time prior to that fatal walk putting up the wire (which he had never bothered with before), worrying about the guidewires and calculating the wind, which he had also never done before.[4]

Doubt can be just as deadly to our spiritual lives. Confidence—not in ourselves but in the work of Christ—is essential. We come to the Father empowered to pray because God has granted us access to Himself through the blood of Jesus Christ. Enjoy your access. After all, it cost our Savior His life.

Don't be afraid to use what Christ has provided for you. James said, "You do not have because you do not ask" (James 4:2). That doesn't grant us liberty to ask for just anything. James also reminded us that we can asl "amiss" (v. 3). But if we believe that what we request of God is within His will, we can boldly go to Him and confidently ask that He provide it. That's the new confidence we have as a Christian.

When we step into God's winner's circle, we join a special group of people. We are more than temporal conquerors; we are eternal winners. We are in the process of being changed into the image of Christ and

76

have been given the privilege of boldly coming to God in prayer about anything we need, anything that troubles us, anything that He wills—anything at all.

But there's more. As winners in the eyes of God we also have:

A new realization

Genesis 32:30 says, "And Jacob called the name of the place Peniel: 'For I have seen God face to face, and my life is preserved.'" Can you detect a note of surprise in this statement? Jacob truly didn't expect to walk away from his wrestling match with God. But he did, and that experience awakened a new realization in him. He saw God from a new perspective – a perspective that reveals:

God's restraint

Maybe you have read the story of Jacob's wrestling match and wondered about this verse: "Now when He [the Angel of the Lord] saw that He did not prevail against him, He touched the socket of his hip; and the socket of Jacob's hip was out of joint as He wrestled with him" (Gen. 32:25). How could a supernatural creature not prevail over a mere mortal like Jacob? There's only one logical answer: because He chose not to.

God is sovereign, but His sovereignty is not out of control. He exercises a measured use of His sovereign power. He doesn't overwhelm us, even though He could if He desired. In salvation, He calls us, woos us, invites us to Him, but He doesn't demand us to respond. Jesus said, "Come to Me, all you who labor and are heavy laden, and I will give you rest" (Matt. 11:28). Elsewhere he said, "O Jerusalem, Jerusalem, the one who kills the prophets and stones those who are sent to her! How often I wanted to gather your children together, as a hen gathers her chicks under her wings, but you were not willing!" (Matt. 23:37). God graciously shows His restraint by not forcing us to come to Him.

There are no robots in God's family. We are not Christians because we were forced or programmed to respond in a particular way. We were drawn by the Spirit of God, and when our spiritual eyes were enlightened, we yielded to the grace of God, the death of Jesus Christ and the wooing of the Holy Spirit. When we wrestle with God, it's only to make us face the issues, not force a decision.

God's instruction

Jacob also came to realize that God uses His sovereign power to mentor, not to crush. When you get in the ring with God, He doesn't have you there to defeat you but to teach you how to fight.

We hear a lot about mentoring these days. Yale professor James Comer says, "Many people refer to mentors and role models as if the terms are synonymous, but they're not. A role model can be anyone a young person chooses to emulate—whether or not the two are personally acquainted. A mentor has a more specific and personal function: to help a younger person learn the ropes by providing guidance and support."[5]

Michael Maya Charles, writing in *Flying* magazine about aviation mentorship, notes, "In ancient tribal cultures, it was the elders, the wise ones, who initiated the younger ones into the adult world." In *Iron John, A*

Book About Men, Robert Bly adds, "The ritual societies believed that a boy becomes a man only through the 'active intervention' of the older men. Mentors in those ancient tribes provided a positive example of how to be— more important than how to do."

God was teaching the selfish Jacob something about himself, not something about wrestling. The only way you can lose with God is to walk away from a wrestling match without having learned anything. When you're wrestling with God about something in your life, don't walk away from the ring without walking away wiser. If you walk away wiser, you always walk away a winner.

Winner takes all

Have you ever played a game in which everybody who plays contributes a certain amount to a common fund (sometimes called a "purse" or a "kitty")? The one who wins gets to take the whole amount; nothing is held back.

When we step into God's winner's circle, the same is true. Nothing is held back. God gives without reservation to conform us to the image of His dear Son. He develops within us a new character, a new confidence and a new realization that we step into each new day with a fabulous opportunity to learn from One who is the fountain of all wisdom.

Coaches counsel their teams with the admonition, "It's not whether you win or lose that counts, but how you play the game." We also frequently hear the reminder, "Winning isn't everything." Yet when it comes to spiritual matters, winning *is* everything! It is important whether you win or lose. In God's game the winner takes all. Choose the winning way. Live life God's way and be a real winner!

---

1 In 1 Kings 18:36, 1 Chronicles 29:18 and 2 Chronicles 30:6, God is referred to as the "God of Abraham, Isaac and Israel" (Jacob's name given after his wrestling match at Peniel).

2 *Jacob* is *yak-ak-obe´*, or "heel-catcher" (i.e., "supplanter"). The name comes from *aw-kab´*, which means to "swell out or up"; used figuratively to mean to "circumvent" (as if tripping up the heels); also to "restrain" (as if holding by the heel), "take by the heel," "stay" or "supplant."

3 When Jacob was born, he came forth and took hold of Esau's heel (Gen. 25:26).

4 H. Edwin Young, "Building blocks," *Southern Baptist Preaching Today*, ed. Allen and Gregory, p. 457.

5 James P. Comer, M.D., "Someone to look up to," *Parents*, November 1991, p. 249.

Chapter 8

CHOOSING THE SACRIFICIAL WAY

On July 27, 1995, a monument depicting 19 American infantrymen arrayed for combat was dedicated in memory of the 54,246 Americans killed in the Korean War between 1950 and 1953. These men and women were willing to sacrifice the most important thing they had—their lives—for the sake of their country.

The same has been true of God's people through the centuries. According to tradition, all the apostles except John were martyred for their faith. Most accounts say that Matthew was slain with a sword in Ethiopia. Peter was crucified upside down at Rome. James the Greater was beheaded at Jerusalem. James the Lesser was thrown from a lofty pinnacle of the temple and then beaten to death with a fuller's club. Philip was hanged up against a pillar at Heiropolis in Phrygia. Bartholomew was flayed alive. Andrew was bound to a cross, where he preached to his persecutors until he died. Thomas was run through the body with a lance at Coromandel in the East Indies. Jude was shot to death with arrows. Matthias (who was elected to take Judas' place) was first stoned and then beheaded.

Others whom we know from the New Testament accounts made similar sacrifices for the sake of the Gospel. Barnabas was stoned to death by the Jews at Salonica. Mark died at Alexandria after having been cruelly dragged through the city streets. Luke was hanged upon an olive tree in Greece. Paul, after various tortures and persecutions, was beheaded at Rome by Emperor Nero.

Nor are these sacrifices a thing of the past. According to Christian Solidarity International, more Christians have been murdered for their faith in the 20th century than in all other centuries combined. More than 150,000 Christians are martyred every year, and nearly two-thirds of the world's population live in countries where Christians are persecuted.[1]

But Jacob was a different story. He was not willing to make the ultimate sacrifice, at least at this point in his life. Genesis 33:1-2 says, "Now Jacob lifted his eyes and looked, and there, Esau was coming, and with him were four hundred men. So he divided the children among Leah, Rachel, and the two maidservants. And he put the maidservants and their children in front, Leah and her children behind, and Rachel and Joseph last."

The sun was up, and from the cloud of dust in the distance Jacob knew that his brother was coming with 400 men. That was a significant threat to Jacob because he had cheated Esau every chance he had. Jacob had a good idea how he would feel if he were in Esau's place—and it wouldn't be very charitable. Consequently, we see a lingering tinge of his selfishness come out in the first verses of chapter 33. In spite of the fact that he had just wrestled with God, Jacob still had selfish instincts. He wanted to be sure not to lose Joseph, his favorite son, and Rachel, his favorite wife. So he assigned values to his family. He decided he would send the two handmaidens and their children first toward Esau. They were the most expendable. Then he would send Leah, the wife he wasn't too keen about anyway. Then he would send

Rachel and finally Joseph. Those he valued least he placed first because the degree of danger was higher.

If you follow college football you might understand the principle of the depth chart. Behind the starting running back is the second-string running back. There's probably a third-string and a fourth-string also; that's the depth chart. The star running back of the University of Nebraska in 1995 was removed from the team after the second game because of unacceptable behavior off the field. So the coach had to go to his depth chart. He went to the back-up running back, and in the first game he played (the third game of the season) the second-string running back was injured. So the next game the coach had to go to the third running back and he, too, was injured. By the fifth game of the season, the coach had gone all the way to the fourth man on the depth chart, which is pretty far down. But the fourth running back rushed for more than 1,000 yards in the remaining games, and Nebraska won its second straight national championship.

In football, you put your best up front. It's risky because of potential injuries, but you always start your best. Jacob, however, was not willing to take that risk. Instead, he put the maidservants and children first, so in case Esau was still very angry with him, he would at least preserve his favorite wife and his favorite son. He operated off a reverse depth chart, wanting to keep the best for himself. Obviously, he was still struggling with selfishness. His selfishness caused him to:

Show favoritism

How would you like to have been Zilpah at this point? Zilpah was Leah's handmaid, and since Leah was not Jacob's favorite wife, presumably Zilpah was not the favorite handmaid. My guess is that Zilpah went first with her children, Gad, Asher, Issachar and Zepulun. Then after Zilpah came Bilhah, Rachel's handmaid, and her sons, Dan and Naphatali. Then followed Leah, his unwanted wife, and her sons, Reuben, Levi, Simeon and Judah. Finally, bringing up the rear was Rachel with Jacob's favorite son, Joseph. This is not family values; this is a family devalued.

Placing different values on various family members is dangerous. If you value one family member over another, you are playing with fire. Jacob knew what it was like, because all the way back to the point of his birth his father, Isaac, loved Esau but his mother, Rebekah, loved him (Gen. 25:28). Jacob came by this favoritism naturally, and it continued in the next generation. Jacob had 12 sons, but his favorite, Joseph, had dreams in which he saw his mother and father and all his brothers bowing down to him. This caused his other brothers to become jealous and angry. That means three generations were affected by parents selfishly playing favorites among their children.

Does this ever happen today? Do parents fail to recognize that when you play favorites in the family, you're laying the foundation for problems that may extend over several generations? It certainly does! When God created us, He created every one of us differently. Children are extremely different, and if you have more than one child in your family you'll agree. Linda and I have four children. One of our children is very tenderhearted, but not particularly organized. Another child is intellectual and very organized. A third child is more people-oriented and easily swayed, while the fourth is strongly opinionated and not easily swayed. Four children who have the same two parents but four very distinct personalities. It would have been easy for us as parents to be attracted to one personality more than another. We could have selfishly chosen to place a higher value on one than on the others. But Linda and I chose to love all four of them because of their differences, not because they were the same. It would have been a monotonous life growing up in the Kroll family if all our kids behaved the same.

We also had creative love for each child because they were different personalities. There were no favorites, even though every one of them was convinced and told the others that they were the favorite in the family. That's the way it should be. Each child should feel special and all of them should feel loved.

If you're playing favorites, stop for a moment and contemplate the problems you're creating for future generations. Consider how the ones who are not your favorite must feel. Think of how selfishly you're behaving. There is no place for favorites in raising a family. Favoritism fosters a fractured family, and nowhere do we see this truth more clearly illustrated than in the saga of Jacob.

Show disrespect

Unwittingly, perhaps, Jacob was communicating an attitude of disrespect toward his brother. As he placed in the forefront those who meant the least to him, he was saying, "OK, Esau, if you have to take out your wrath on someone, here are my least-valued family members. Do what you want with them, but don't harm the people I really value."

This was God's complaint in the Book of Malachi. He said,

> A son honors his father, and a servant his master. If then I am the Father, where is My honor? And if I am a Master, where is My reverence? says the LORD of hosts to you priests who despise My name. Yet you say, "In what way have we despised Your name?" You offer defiled food on My altar. But you say, "In what way have we defiled You?" By saying, "The table of the LORD is contemptible." And when you offer the blind as a sacrifice, is it not evil? And when you offer the lame and sick, is it not evil? Offer it then to your governor! Would he be pleased with you? Would he accept you favorably? says the LORD of hosts (Mal. 1:6-8).

The people were bringing their rejects, their leftovers, the things they valued least, and were offering them to God. But He said, "Not even an earthly governor would stand for such disrespect." God will not settle for the crumbs from our table. He will never be pleased if we give Him our least and selfishly keep the best for ourselves.

Have you given your family to God? Have you given *all* of them to God, or are you holding back a favorite son or daughter for fear God might call him or her away from you? Are you offering to God what's least important to you in hopes that He might be satisfied with that and not ask for what is most important? Has the Church offered the world of science and technology our best and brightest young people and encouraged those we didn't think would make it in the world to consider lifetime ministry?

Hallmark Cards® had the slogan, "When you care enough to send the best." That's what Christians need to do. We must send our very best. What we give is an indication of how much we love and respect the One who receives our gift. For God, it should be the very best that we have.

The supreme example

For a man who had met God face to face, Jacob had a lot to learn about sacrifice. So do most of the rest of us. If we take an honest look at ourselves, we'd have to agree with Jacob Stam, whose brother John, a missionary, was martyred in China, when he prayed, "Oh, God, all that most of us know about sacrifice is how to spell the word."

Yet the very focal point of the Gospel is sacrifice. John 3:16 tells us, "For God so loved the world that He *gave* His only begotten Son, that whoever believes in Him should not perish but have everlasting life" (emphasis mine). Even though Jesus was God's only Son, He did not hesitate to offer Him as a sacrifice for our sins. There was no favoritism shown. Some misguided people insist that God only sent an angel—the archangel Michael—as our redeemer. But Scripture says it was "His only begotten Son." Such a sacrifice was done:

Willingly

Oswald Chambers observed, "Our notion of sacrifice is the wringing out of us something we don't want to give up, full of pain and agony and distress. The Bible's idea of sacrifice is that I willingly give the very best thing I have."

No one forced God to give His Son; He did it out of love. Romans 5:8 says, "But God demonstrates His own love toward us, in that while we were still sinners, Christ died for us." It was not nails that kept the Son of God on the cross, but love.

During World War I there was a young French soldier who was seriously wounded. His arm was so badly mangled that it had to be amputated. He was a magnificent specimen of young manhood, and the surgeon was grieved that he must go through life maimed. The doctor waited beside his bedside to tell him the bad news when he recovered consciousness. When the lad's eyes opened, the surgeon said to him, "I am sorry to tell you that you have lost your arm." "Sir," the soldier replied, "I did not lose it; I gave it—for France."

Jesus did not lose His life; He gave it for you and me. The cross was not thrust upon Him; He willingly accepted it—for us.

Unconditionally

I recently did a small favor for a friend. Half-jokingly he replied, "Well, I guess I owe you one." But he doesn't. A true sacrifice is not a debt expected to be repaid; it is a gift given with no strings attached. When Jesus died on the cross, He did not say, "All right, now, if you live up to my expectations you can be saved." Rather He said, "Come to Me, all you who labor and are heavy laden, and I will give you rest. Take My yoke upon you and learn from Me, for I am gentle and lowly in heart, and you will find rest for your souls" (Matt. 11:28-29). The only condition to salvation is faith—faith to trust that what Jesus accomplished on the cross is all that is necessary to purchase our redemption.

God doesn't turn our salvation into a performance contest. Obviously, those who have a renewed heart will have a renewed life. We will want to serve Him. But like Jacob, sometimes it takes a while for us to catch on.

Joyfully

The late Malcom Muggeridge observed, "Christians are often accused of being morbid when they talk of the joy of sacrificing. I think it is one of the deepest truths of the Christian religion. Far from being a source of sadness, sacrifice is a great joy and source of illumination, perhaps the greatest of all."

Charles T. Studd gave himself without reservation to Christ. He was born into a wealthy British family in 1862. He became an outstanding cricket player, most notably at Cambridge University. In his third year at the university he was converted at a Moody-Sankey meeting and dedicated his life to Christ. Shortly thereafter he announced that he was giving away his personal fortune, leaving the world of sports and becoming a missionary to China. Studd explained his motivation in these words: "If Jesus Christ be God and died for me, then no sacrifice that I make can be too great for Him."

Jesus found no regret in His sacrifice. Hebrews 12:2 says that Jesus, "the author and finisher of our faith, who for the *joy* that was set before Him endured the cross, despising the shame, and has sat down at the right hand of the throne of God" (emphasis mine). The joy He knew would come from His sacrifice made it all worthwhile.

Selfishness or sacrifice?

When it comes to lifestyles, there are only two choices: we can live selfishly or we can live sacrificially. One is lived making sure that the things we prize most are reserved for our enjoyment. The other is lived in joyful abandonment to the will of God. Which will it be for you? The joy of sacrifice or the pain of selfishness?

As hymn writer Elisha Hoffman so aptly asked, "Is your all on the altar of sacrifice laid? Your heart does the Spirit control? You can only be blessed and have peace and sweet rest as you yield Him your body and soul."[2]

Jacob lived much of his life in a failing struggle with selfishness. In some respects his was a sad life. If you have come to realize that you, too, are struggling with selfishness, check your family depth chart. Begin by giving yourself, your spouse and your children to the Lord as an expression of love and gratitude. That which we give to Christ is not lost; it is invested. When you give God the best you have, you begin to be freed from the chains of selfishness.

---

1 *National & International Religion Report*, February 20, 1995, Vol. 9, No. 5, p. 7.

2 Elisha A. Hoffman, "Is Your All on the Altar?" *Great Hymns of the Faith* (Grand Rapids, Mich.: Zondervan Publishing House, 1968).

Chapter 9

THE FATAL FLAW OF SELFISHNESS

Why are people selfish? Why do they refuse to make the right choices? Because their thinking is flawed. Flawed thinking is any kind of thinking that does not reflect the eternal purpose or standards of God. People believe by their selfishness they can achieve what they desire and live happily ever after. That type of thinking, however, never accomplishes what it promises.

Jacob's experience

Jacob is one of the premier biblical examples of this kind of thought process. His selfishness got him what he wanted, but it didn't make him happy. In fact, selfishly getting what he wanted made him terribly unhappy. Genesis 25:34 says, "And Jacob gave Esau bread and stew of lentils; then he ate and drank, arose, and went his way. Thus Esau despised his birthright." But after Jacob stole the blessing from his brother, the Bible also says, "So Esau hated Jacob because of the blessing with which his father blessed him, and Esau said in his heart, 'The days of mourning for my father are at hand; then I will kill my brother Jacob'" (Gen. 27:41). Jacob lived under a cloud of fear and in the presence of hatred until finally his mother advised him to flee to her brother Laban in Haran. There she thought Jacob would remain only "a few days" until Esau's anger had passed. Rebekah's "few days," however, turned into an exile of 20 years and she never saw her son again. Jacob paid a very high price, and his selfishness didn't bring lasting happiness.

Nor was the time spent with his Uncle Laban a joyful experience. Listen in on Jacob's complaint of his uncle's treatment of him:

> These twenty years I have been with you; your ewes and your female goats have not miscarried their young, and I have not eaten the rams of your flock. That which was torn by beasts I did not bring to you; I bore the loss of it. You required it from my hand, whether stolen by day or stolen by night. There I was! In the day the drought consumed me, and the frost by night, and my sleep departed from my eyes. Thus I have been in your house twenty years; I served you fourteen years for your two daughters, and six years for your flock, and you have changed my wages ten times. Unless the God of my father, the God of Abraham and the Fear of Isaac, had been with me, surely now you would have sent me away empty-handed (Gen. 31:38-42).

Jacob was a fugitive, an exile, the servant of an uncle who was just as crooked as he was—all because of selfishness. Once we view selfishness through God's eyes, we see the price paid for a selfish attitude is far too high. The saga of Jacob proves that.

Lot's experience

Yet Jacob was not the first victim of flawed thinking. The story of Lot depicts the deadly results of a selfish soul. Abraham, called Abram at this point, was very rich in livestock, silver and gold. When he pitched his tent between Bethel and Ai, the land was not sufficiently verdant to support both his large herds and those of his nephew Lot. Abraham suggested that each of them choose a portion of the land. Genesis 13:10-13 says,

> And Lot lifted his eyes and saw all the plain of Jordan, that it was well watered everywhere (before the LORD destroyed Sodom and Gomorrah) like the garden of the LORD, like the land of Egypt as you go toward Zoar. Then Lot chose for himself all the plain of Jordan, and Lot journeyed east. And they separated from each other. Abram dwelt in the land of Canaan, and Lot dwelt in the cities of the plain and pitched his tent even as far as Sodom. But the men of Sodom were exceedingly wicked and sinful against the LORD.

Abraham was the uncle; Lot the nephew. Abraham was the elder; Lot the junior. Abraham was the more wealthy; Lot the less wealthy. In essence, Abraham said to Lot, "Look, you and I can't exist together here because the land just won't support both of us with our vast holdings. So what I'd like you to do is look around and choose one part of the country, and I'll choose another part of the country. We'll go our separate ways and God will bless both of us." It was a logical plan. And then

Abraham, being the consummate gentleman, said to Lot, "Which would you like?"

The moment of truth arrived. Lot had first pick. Consumed with selfishness, he looked around and said, "I'll take the best." That was flawed thinking. He didn't realize that Abraham was graciously giving him the opportunity to take what God had assigned to him. Selfishness drove his choice to settle on the well-watered plains. Unfortunately, the well-watered plains just happened to include the cities of Sodom and Gomorrah, where the men "were exceedingly wicked and sinful against the LORD." This selfish choice brought Lot down and created a life of unhappiness.

I wish Abraham had jumped in and said, "Lot, thanks for your choice, but you need to stay out of Sodom and Gomorrah." But he didn't. Lot's flawed thinking wasn't corrected and it led to the rest of the story. In Genesis 13:10 we find Lot looking at Sodom from afar. In verse 12 he pitched his tents close to Sodom. And by the time we reach Genesis 19, Lot was living in Sodom. In fact, Genesis 19:1 places Lot "sitting in the gate of Sodom," the place of authority, honor and leadership. Lot may have moved into Sodom to be a witness, but he became a ringleader.

Selfishness made Lot's thinking so flawed that when he gave refuge to two angels who came to Sodom and the town mob demanded Lot release them so they could engage in a night of homosexuality, unbelievably, Lot countered with this offer, "Please, my brethren, do not do so wickedly! See now, I have two daughters who have not known a man; please, let me bring them out to you, and you may do to them as you wish; only do nothing to these men, since this is the reason they have come under the shadow of my roof'" (vv. 7-8). A man's thinking can't get much more flawed than that!

Lot was a just man, a godly man, but selfishness had so twisted his thinking that, influenced by the environment in which he lived, he offered his two daughters to be abused by these men if they would just not commit their despicable acts of homosexuality. How foolish! As if God would be pleased by trading one heinous sin for another. This wasn't just warped thinking—it was immoral thinking, and it's the kind of thinking we progress to when flawed thinking is not intercepted early and corrected. Is it any wonder that after Lot and his family escaped from Sodom his flawed thinking led to one further step? Living with their father's flawed thinking led Lot's two daughters to decide committing incest with their father was better than remaining childless. Genesis 19 records that the result of their flawed reasoning was Moab and Ben-Ammi, sons from whom came two great peoples (the Moabites and Ammonites) and the two constant enemies who plagued Israel throughout history. Not only had Lot moved into Sodom, but Sodom had moved into Lot, and the consequences passed from one generation to the next.

The fruit of selfishness

Selfishness sows seeds that will grow up one day to ruin you. If there's something for us to learn from Jacob, it is this: When someone comes to us with a need and it's in our power to meet that need but we selfishly refuse, or they come to us with a need and we immorally make a demand on them before we will meet that need, or when they come to us and we see their flawed thinking but don't correct them because we selfishly see it as an opportunity to advance ourselves, the result is often tragedy—not their tragedy but ours. Selfishness results in hurt—not their hurt nearly as much as our hurt.

Ernest Hooten was born in 1887. He was a physical anthropologist at Harvard University. Perhaps Dr. Hooten is best remembered for his statement about selfishness. He said, "Man is still a super-age savage, predatory, acquisitive, primarily interested in himself. And what you and I are naturally, my friends, is exactly the opposite of what Jesus supernaturally saved us to be." Given the fact that God spared not His own Son but freely and unselfishly offered Him as an atonement for our sins, the words "selfish Christian" should be an oxymoron. These two words should never fit together but, unfortunately, often they do.

In 281 B.C. the people of Tarentum, a Greek colony in southern Italy, were at war with the Romans. The people sent a plea to Pyrrhus, king of Epirus, to come and help them. Early in 280 B.C. he sailed for Tarentum with a force of 25,000 men and 20 elephants. He met and defeated the Romans at Heraclea but with a tremendous loss among his own army. He reportedly responded, "Another such victory over the Romans, and we are undone." As a result, today we refer to a victory achieved at an excessive cost as a pyrrhic victory.

Surely selfishness falls into this category. When we act selfishly we may gain what we crave so intensely, but the price will be incredibly high—too high. If you must compromise your morality, your honesty, your intimacy and your blessing in the process of winning, is it really a victory? Selfishness destroys the soul while winning the substance. What do you want so terribly that it is worth destroying your soul for? How do you answer Jesus' poignant question, "What good is it for a man to gain the whole world, yet forfeit his soul?" (Mark 8:36). Such a "victory" would be, in reality, a devastating defeat.

Wouldn't it be wonderful if receiving Christ as Savior put an end to all selfish behavior? It certainly would, but that doesn't happen. On numerous occasions Paul warned Christians to beware of selfish attitudes that could slip into their thinking. He commanded the Corinthian Christians, "Let no one seek his own, but each one the other's well-being" (1 Cor. 10:24). He felt constrained to repeat this command in Galatians 6:2 with the instructions, "Bear one another's burdens, and so fulfill the law of Christ." Even the beloved church at Philippi was exhorted, "Let nothing be done through selfish ambition or conceit, but in lowliness of mind let each esteem others better than himself" (Phil. 2:3).

But God's Word not only points out the problem, it also provides the solution, as we'll see next.

Conclusion

THE ULTIMATE SOLUTION

The beginning point of any change is found in a personal encounter with Jesus Christ. While we may try to alter some outward behavior, Christ goes to the heart of the problem—the heart itself. Jesus said, "For out of the heart proceed evil thoughts, murders, adulteries, fornications, thefts, false witness, blasphemies" (Matt. 15:19). No wonder a changed life begins with a changed heart.

Jacob came to the point where his life was turned around, and it all started when he wrestled the Angel of the Lord. In a solitary place he later called Peniel ("For I have seen God face to face, and my life is preserved"), the patriarch pitted his strength against a supernatural visitor. He could not win—but he could cling. His perseverance won him a new heart and a new name. The Angel said, "Your name shall no longer be called Jacob, but Israel; for you have struggled with God and with men, and have prevailed" (Gen. 32:28).

But Jacob had a difficult journey ahead. When he limped away from that wrestling match, his life was not over. In fact, it was really just beginning. Genesis 33 records Jacob's reunion with his estranged twin brother, Esau. Instead of the fierce battle that Jacob feared, the two men, both now about 60 years old, began hugging one another and crying. Both of them knew their lives had been changed. They weren't the same battling brothers they were two decades earlier. But in the years ahead, Jacob would travel from the Promised Land down into Egypt, experience problems with his children and face numerous other trials. In spite of the fact that he was on the right road, lots of life's up and downs still lay before him. God knew Jacob needed some preparation for his journey from selfishness to selflessness.

That preparation is revealed to us in Genesis 35:1-4:

> God said to Jacob, "Arise, go up to Bethel and dwell there; and make an altar there to God, who appeared to you when you fled from the face of Esau your brother." And Jacob said to his household and to all who were with him, "Put away the foreign gods that are among you, purify yourselves, and change your garments. Then let us arise and go up to Bethel; and I will make an altar there to God, who answered me in the day of my distress and has been with me in the way which I have gone." So they gave Jacob all the foreign gods which were in their hands, and the earrings which were in their ears; and Jacob hid them under the terebinth tree which was by Shechem.

Jacob's journey would take the rest of his life. During this time he would struggle with selfishness—sometimes winning the struggle, sometimes losing. But we gain valuable insight into our own struggle with selfishness by taking note of the specific actions Jacob took when he began to walk with God. These are the same actions we must take when we decide to turn from selfishness and walk with God. A changed heart was only the beginning, as Jacob discovered.

Over the years we all learn many selfish habits. In fact, our society encourages selfishness. Shirley MacLaine, the award-winning actress, spoke for the majority when she told a *Washington Post* interviewer in 1977, "The most pleasurable journey you take is through yourself—the only sustaining love is with yourself. When you look back on your life and try to figure out where you've been and where you're going, when you look at your work, your love affairs, your marriages, your children, your pain, your happiness—when you examine all that closely, what you really find out is that the only person you really go to bed with is yourself. The only thing you have is working to the consummation of your own identity."

MacLaine's rather skewed view of life is starkly different from Jesus' view. He instructed us, "If anyone desires to come after Me, let him deny himself, and take up his cross, and follow Me. For whoever desires to save his life will lose it, but whoever loses his life for My sake will find it" (Matt. 16:24-25). To live this kind of life when most people buy into Shirley MacLaine's view of life, you need a unique preparation. If you've been struggling with selfishness and want to start over as Jacob did, follow his lead.

Listen for God's call

To turn from selfishness and walk with God requires listening for and responding to His call on our life. God called Jacob to "arise and go to Bethel and dwell there." Now that Jacob had a new heart, God had a new plan for his life. God didn't tell him all the details, but He told Jacob enough for him to know what he needed to do. The distant future was not clear, but Jacob knew what had to be done today—"arise and go." That was God's voice telling Jacob what to do next. Jacob now had a direction and a goal.

How about you? Do you know why you're saved? If you're a Christian there's a purpose for your life. Perhaps you've heard me say that you should never quote Ephesians 2:8-9 without quoting verse 10. That verse tells us why verses 8-9 are important. We are saved "by grace through faith," but verse 10 tells us why. "For we are His workmanship, created in Christ Jesus for good works, which God prepared beforehand that we should walk in them."

God's purpose in saving you is to enable you to answer His call on your life. He didn't save you just so you could escape hell. In fact, escaping hell is only half the purpose of salvation. Titus 2:14 tells us that Jesus "gave Himself for us, that He might redeem us from every lawless deed and purify for Himself His own special people, zealous for good works." All of us who receive Jesus as Savior go to heaven when we die—not because of anything we've done but because of what Jesus did for us. But there's more to it than that.

Our salvation gets us into heaven, but why aren't we there now? If heaven is so great—and it is—why doesn't Jesus take us there as soon as we are saved? Why has He left us here? The answer is in Genesis 35:1—God has a call on your life. He has left you and me here to fulfill His purpose in our lives.

I can't tell you specifically what the call of God is on your life, but I do know that He has a plan for whatever days you have left. The most miserable people on the face of the earth are not unbelievers. Most of them don't have a clue what awaits them. No, the most miserable people on earth are believers who are here and don't know why. They haven't answered the call of God on their lives.

When Steve Jobs, the founder of Apple Computers®, was attempting to recruit John Sculley, the 38-year-old president of Pepsi-Cola®, Jobs asked Sculley this penetrating question: "Do you want to spend the rest of your life selling sugared water, or do you want a chance to change the world?"

That challenge got Sculley to leave Pepsi-Cola and join Apple. Maybe that's God's challenge to you. What do you want to do with the rest of your life? I've mentored students for almost 20 years as a university professor and later as president of Practical Bible College. During that time I learned never to make it easy for students. They need to be challenged. Often I would ask, "What's the last thing you want to do before you die?" I suppose I've asked that question hundreds of times, but no one has ever answered me. But that's an important question. How would you answer it? Knowing what you want to do before you die affects tomorrow. Since you don't how many days you have left, you need to get to it right away. Regardless of your age, you have relatively little time left.

In an article entitled "If You Are 35, You Have 500 Days to Live,"[1] the author subtracted the time spent sleeping, working, eating, traveling and tending to personal matters, hygiene, odd chores, medical matters and miscellaneous time-stealers. Assuming you live to be 71 years old, he claims you will have roughly the equivalent of 500 days left to spend as you wish. Of course, you cannot be assured of reaching 71, but if you did, you still have little time. If Jesus felt that He must work because "the night is coming when no one can work" (John 9:4), shouldn't we share His perspective?

Moving away from selfishness and into a life that is meaningful and fulfilling requires that we respond to God's calling on our life. Doing what God has called us to do is the most pleasurable thing in life. It brings a peace that others never experience. There isn't a Christian alive today who doesn't have the call of God on his or her life. The question is, "Do you know what it is and have you answered it?"

Give up your idols

There is more preparatory work to be done in our journey out of selfishness. Jacob said to his household and all who were with him, "Put away the foreign gods that are among you" (Gen. 35:2). Man is a religious creature. He *will* worship something. If he refuses to worship the true God, he will worship something or someone else. Whatever he chooses to worship other than God is an idol.

Archaeologists tell us that during the days of the apostle Paul there were more than 3,000 public statues in Athens representing either a god or a hero. When Rome conquered Greece, the cultural center of the ancient world, the Romans said, "It is easier to find a god than a man in Athens." The situation was no better in Jacob's time. God was teaching Jacob that it was impossible for him to hang on to things that were more precious to him than God and find his way back to Him at the same time.

You can't answer God's call on your life and begin your journey away from selfishness until you're willing to give up your idols. Some idols are made of stone, wood or metal. You likely don't have many of those. But other idols can be good things simply used wrongly. Your idol may be your business. It may consume all your time and your energy. It may be driving a wedge between your spouse and you. It may be the most important thing in your life—and that's what makes it an idol. Maybe sports is your idol. Many people have made idols out of athletes. They exert such an influence over us that whatever product they are hawking on television is the product we buy, even if they have only memorized a script and know virtually nothing of the product they advertise. On the other hand, your idol could be your education. I've spent a great deal of my life around people who idolize education. They assign everyone to a social caste based on the amount of education they possess. But education is only a tool, not an end. It's what God gives you so you can answer His call and be used of Him more effectively.

An interesting development during the last few years is that some people have made their family their idol. We hear a lot about family values these days, and we should. For years many people, including many Christians, placed little emphasis on families as they busily pursued a career and the good life. Their families suffered as a result. This now seems to be changing for the better, but we must be cautious. If we put family before God, that makes them our idol. Jesus said, "He who loves father or mother more than Me is not worthy of Me. And he who loves son or daughter more than Me is not worthy of Me" (Matt. 10:37). Naturally, your family should be very important to you and right behind God on your list of priorities; but anything that hinders you from full obedience to God is an idol, even the good things. When family concerns and desires replace God's concerns and desires, you need to put away your idols. We can't simply put away our families as we can other idols, but when families draw us into sin, all who would live godly lives must walk away. Sometimes it's a tough choice, but any choice but God is the wrong choice.

Clean lives

If a man is going to walk with God, he must also be clean. He has to sanctify himself. The Hebrew language uses the word *taher* for sanctify. It means "to be bright" or, by implication, "to be pure, clear, unadulterated." God accepts only servants who have clean hands and a pure heart.

I'm frequently asked in interviews with the media, "What do you think is the greatest need in the church today?" I know they expect me to say the church needs revival or the church needs evangelism. It is certainly true; the church does need revival and we will never win the world to Christ until we take evangelism more seriously. But I don't think either of these is the greatest need of the church.

No, I believe the greatest need in the church today is the need for purity. When you look at the bottom line, what churches need most today is saints with cleansed lives, men and women who can stand blameless before God and the world. Jacob realized that if he answered the call of God and put away his idols, he and his family still needed to be morally clean. I say without reservation that the most important need in my life, if I am to be used at Back to the Bible to teach the Word and touch the world, is not a better understanding of God's Word, nor more hours spent in preparation, or even more skill in the studio. The most important thing in my life is that I am clean before God. I must be blameless before the Lord and a watching world.

That doesn't mean sinless; I won't be sinless this side of heaven. But I must be blameless, with clean hands and a pure heart. I must keep short accounts with God and confess my sins genuinely and often. And what is true for me if I want to walk with God is also true for you.

First John 1:9 says, "If we confess our sins, He is faithful and just to forgive us our sins and to cleanse us from all unrighteousness." To confess means to "agree with God." God can't forgive us for a sin that we deny is a sin. But when we are willing to drag out our dirty laundry, hang it up before the Lord and admit that it is offensive to Him, He promises to cleanse us. Before God can use us to accomplish His purpose in our lives, we have to be made clean. If there is something in your life that you know will keep God from using you as you would like, admit that it is sin. Agree with what God says about it in His Word. Ask Him to forgive you of it and have strong confidence in the fact that "the blood of Jesus Christ His Son cleanses us from all sin" (1 John 1:8). The journey out of selfishness requires cleansing, and that requires a shower from the blood of the Savior.

New habits

Selfishness is a habit and, as we all know, habits are harder to break than to form. During the time we were under Satan's tutelage, he taught us how to respond selfishly. Now that we're under the management of the Holy Spirit, we have to learn a new response.

In Genesis 35:2, Jacob instructed his household to change their garments. Our clothing is what people see of us outwardly. They can't see our hearts, but they can see how we dress. When Jacob's family put on fresh garments, they were symbolizing that they intended to respond in a new way. They put away their old, unclean habits—as they did their old garments—and took fresh, clean ones to themselves.

Anybody who is going to progress with God, who has cleared his account with God and his brother, still needs to have a change of garments. That's part of the process of preparation for the journey. So what are these new clothes? First Peter 5:5 speaks of being clothed with humility, and Colossians 3:12 talks about putting on "tender mercies, kindness, humility, meekness and longsuffering." Most importantly, though, we need to put on love (Col. 3:14). These are the new clothes we don when we walk away from the selfishness of our old life. A new man puts on new clothes. When you are a new man, you want to look like it too.

As a new battle needs new battle gear, a new career needs a new wardrobe, so a new spiritual life needs new habits. Ephesians 6 talks about girding our waist with truth, putting on the breastplate of righteousness and having our feet shod with the preparation of the gospel of peace. And don't forget to accessorize—with the shield of faith, the helmet of salvation and the sword of the Spirit, which is the Word of God. We even need new traveling clothes because we're traveling to a new destination with a new climate. When we arrive in heaven we'll be wrapped in the new garments of the blood of Jesus Christ and His righteousness.

When you move on with God after a long and difficult wrestling match with Him, you need to put on new clothes—not just something you got off the rack, but something washed in the blood of Jesus Christ and made white as a pure linen garment.

So how do people see you dressed? Are you garbed in selfishness, or do they see your old clothes have been replaced with new clothes because you have been washed and made ready to travel with God?

The choice is yours

The journey is a long one. In fact, it will take the rest of your life. Along the way you will be faced with many choices. Sometimes you will be forced to choose between what's morally right and what's simply expedient. At times you may be required to swim against the tide of dishonesty by making honest choices. Walking with God will bring you into conflict with those who have chosen unrighteousness as their pathway. In humility and frequently in solitude, you will have to stand against the majority opinion. Your choices may mean sacrificing financial gains and a comfortable life. You may even lose some friendships. Yet as you stand in the winner's circle surrounding God's heavenly throne and worshipfully cast your crowns at His feet, it will be worth it all.

So what will it be? The old Jacob—selfish, on the run, constantly cheating and being cheated? Or the new Jacob—forgiven, fulfilled, following God? The choice is yours. Allow Jacob's saga to guide your choices. The struggle with selfishness will not be easy; old habits die hard. But the struggle to be free from selfish behavior is a struggle worth pursuing. God can give you the victory. Make the right choice. Follow God's way.

1 Tim Hansel, *When I Relax I Feel Guilty* (Elgin, Ill.: David C. Cook, 1979).

Back to the Bible is a nonprofit ministry dedicated to Bible teaching, evangelism and edification of Christians worldwide.

If we may assist you in knowing more about Christ and the Christian life, please write to us without obligation.

Back to the Bible
P.O. Box 82808
Lincoln, NE 68501